From Perfectionism to Happiness

The Complete Guide to Reduced Anxiety, Improved Time Management, Self-Compassion and Better Relationships

Claudia Turcotte

Contents

About the author

Claudia Turcotte is a passionate advocate for emotional wellness, a devoted mother of two and an author committed to helping families and individuals thrive. Building on her studies in psychology and social work (Master's and Bachelor's), along with a certification in Energy Coaching and specialized training in emotional management, Claudia offers practical tools to lighten life's burdens and nurture emotional resilience.

As a coach, Claudia draws on both her personal and professional experiences to empower people to cultivate emotional well-being and build fulfilling lives. Driven by a desire to make emotional health accessible, her mission is simple yet profound: to support parents, children, and adults in mastering their emotions so everyone can experience a lighter, more vibrant life. Her approachable style and genuine enthusiasm make her work both relatable and transformative, ensuring that no matter where you are on your journey, you'll find the guidance and inspiration you need to flourish.

As a gifted adult raising gifted children, she has gained unique insights into navigating intense emotions, heightened sensitivity, and a variety of challenges. Passionate about the topic of giftedness for more than a decade, Claudia is dedicated to supporting parents and adults on their giftedness journey, helping them feel empowered and confident as they navigate the unique challenges and opportunities that come with their traits.

Introduction

Y ou're at work, staring at a blank document on your computer screen. The deadline is looming, but you can't seem to get started. You want it to be perfect and flawless, but the pressure is paralyzing. This struggle isn't just at work; it spills into your relationships, self-image, and even your free time. Sound familiar? If it does, you're not alone. Many of us wrestle with the relentless pursuit of perfection, often to our detriment.

This book is about turning perfectionism into a balanced pursuit of happiness and contentment. It's not just a lofty idea; it's a necessary shift for a fulfilling life. This journey isn't about eliminating your drive for excellence. Instead, it's about transforming it into something healthier and more sustainable. You'll find practical steps and real-life examples to guide you through this transformation.

The purpose of this book is to provide practical strategies for managing perfectionism. We'll focus on fostering self-compassion, improving relationships, and enhancing overall well-being. Perfectionism can affect many areas of life—your career, personal relationships, and even how you see yourself. Each chapter will build on the previous one, walking you through understanding, managing, and eventually thriving beyond perfectionism.

I know this journey well because I've lived it. My own struggles and the lessons I've learned form the backbone of this book. I've experienced the toll that perfectionism can take and have found ways to move beyond it. I hope these insights will resonate with you and provide the support you need.

This book takes a unique approach to tackling perfectionism. We'll use real-life applications and the CALM method to make these concepts memorable and actionable. CALM stands for Capture your thoughts, Accept imperfections, Let go of control, and Mindfulness practice. These elements are designed to provide clear, practical advice you can implement in your daily life.

You're about to embark on a transformative experience. This book doesn't just address the challenges of perfectionism; it offers a roadmap to a happier, more balanced life. Each chapter builds on the last, creating a comprehensive guide to embracing imperfection.

This book is for anyone who feels trapped by the pursuit of perfection. Whether you're a student, a professional, or someone struggling in personal relationships, this book is for you. It's written in a way that is accessible to everyone, regardless of where you are in your journey.

I invite you to start this journey with an open mind and a willingness to challenge your beliefs about perfectionism and success. The path may not be easy, but the outcome—true happiness and self-acceptance—is worth the effort. The real power of this book lies in your commitment to applying the lessons and strategies provided. Every step you take toward embracing imperfection is a step toward a more fulfilling life.

Let's take this journey together. Remember, it's not about being perfect; it's about being happy.

Chapter 1

Understanding Perfectionism

You've just spent hours meticulously planning a dinner party, arranging every detail down to the color of the napkins. Yet, as the evening unfolds, you find yourself unable to enjoy the company of your friends. Instead, you're obsessing over a minor detail you missed—a slightly overcooked dish or a wine glass with a smudge. This isn't about being detail-oriented or striving for excellence; it's about something deeper and more pervasive. This is perfectionism, a relentless drive that can often lead to significant distress and dissatisfaction.

1.1 Defining Perfectionism and Its Psychological Roots

Perfectionism is not merely about having high standards. It's about setting unreasonably high expectations for yourself and others, where anything short of flawless feels like failure. This isn't just being thorough or committed; it's a deeper issue that can lead to significant stress and emotional strain. Perfectionism is often misunderstood as a positive trait, but its darker side can be incredibly damaging, rooted in a powerful fear of failure or disapproval. It involves a harsh self-criticism that leaves little room for mistakes, viewing them not as learning opportunities but as catastrophic failures.

Psychologically, perfectionism has been studied extensively, and several theories explain its origins. Cognitive-behavioral perspectives suggest that perfectionism is rooted in fear—fear of failure and fear of disapproval from others. This fear drives you to overcompensate, to double-check and triple-check every task, often leading to paralysis by analysis. Psychodynamic theories, on the other hand, link perfectionism to issues of self-worth and control. The idea is that you may use perfectionism as a way to feel valuable and in control of your life, compensating for feelings of inadequacy or insecurity.

Anxiety plays a crucial role in perfectionism. The constant need to meet impossibly high standards creates a perpetual state of worry. You might find yourself avoiding tasks or procrastinating because the fear of not doing them perfectly is too overwhelming. This avoidance is not laziness; it's a coping mechanism for managing the anxiety that comes with the possibility of failure. The emotional toll can be immense, leading to chronic stress and even physical symptoms like headaches, digestive issues, and insomnia.

Chronic perfectionism can result in severe mental health issues. The relentless self-criticism and the constant pressure to be perfect can lead to depression, where you might feel a persistent sense of sadness and hopelessness. Anxiety disorders are also common, where the worry about meeting standards or the fear of making mistakes can become debilitating. In some cases, perfectionism can contribute to obsessive-compulsive tendencies, where you might engage in repetitive behaviors or thoughts in an attempt to achieve perfection. The long-term impact on mental health can be profound, affecting your overall well-being and quality of life.

Understanding perfectionism is the first step in managing it. It's not just about being organized or striving for excellence; it's a deeper psychological issue that can have far-reaching consequences on your emotional and mental health. By recognizing the underlying fears and anxieties that drive perfectionism, you can begin to address them and work towards a healthier, more balanced approach to life. This chapter will help you understand these psychological roots, giving you the insight needed to start making meaningful changes.

1.2 The Perfectionism Spectrum: From Healthy to Toxic

Perfectionism isn't a one-size-fits-all trait. It exists on a spectrum, stretching from adaptive ("healthy") to maladaptive ("toxic"). On one end, healthy striving motivates us to push beyond our comfort zones, while on the other, toxic perfectionism traps us in self-criticism. Recognizing these differences allows for excellence without the emotional toll of impossible standards.

Healthy perfectionism, or adaptive striving, is fueled by personal growth rather than fear. Instead of being consumed by a need to avoid mistakes, individuals with this mindset see high standards as a way to improve. They are resilient, flexible, and driven by curiosity rather than anxiety. For example, a writer with healthy perfectionism revises their draft multiple times, not because they fear being inadequate, but because they value refining their craft. An athlete focused on adaptive perfectionism trains diligently, setting challenging yet realistic goals while still celebrating progress along the way.

What sets healthy perfectionists apart is their ability to balance ambition with self-awareness. They push themselves to excel but also recognize when perfectionism is unproductive or even counterproductive. A musician preparing for a performance might strive for technical mastery but still embrace the emotional expression of their piece rather than fixating on every single note. In a professional setting, an entrepreneur with adaptive perfectionism aims for excellence but knows that launching an imperfect product is better than delaying endlessly in pursuit of flawlessness.

This contrasts with toxic perfectionism, which is marked by unrelenting self-criticism and a chronic sense of failure. You might avoid tasks because you fear they won't be perfect, leading to procrastination and burnout. It doesn't just affect work; it spills over into personal life, making it hard to enjoy hobbies or relax. This paralyzing cycle can exhaust your mental and emotional resources, leaving you feeling empty and overwhelmed.

The nature of perfectionism can shift along this spectrum. External pressures like a demanding job or past failures might push you toward the toxic end. In contrast, personal growth and supportive environments can help you adopt a healthier mindset. You could be more balanced at work yet feel toxically perfectionistic in your personal life—or vice versa. This variability shows perfectionism is not static; it evolves as you encounter new challenges and insights.

Recognizing where you fall on this spectrum is the first step in managing perfectionism. Spotting signs of toxic perfectionism—like pervasive self-criticism, chronic dissatisfaction, and avoidance behaviors—is crucial. It helps you intervene early and prevent the negative impacts of toxic perfectionism. Likewise, acknowledging and nurturing healthier tendencies allows you to leverage your high standards in a way that fosters success and well-being. This means celebrating progress, embracing a growth mindset, and setting high but realistic goals. By consciously shifting your approach, you can harness the positive aspects of perfectionism while mitigating its potential harms.

1.3 How Perfectionism Masks Itself as Ambition

Imagine you're working late in an office, the glow of your computer screen the only light in the room. You've convinced yourself that this overtime is a testament to your ambition, a drive to reach the top. But beneath that surface lies a hidden layer of self-doubt, the fear of not being good enough. While ambition is about striving for success, perfectionism is about fearing failure. This distinction matters because ambition can be healthy, whereas perfectionism often feeds anxiety and avoidance.

Our modern work culture often blurs the lines between ambition and perfectionism. Overworking is glorified; long hours are seen as a badge of honor. Think about the corporate environment where employees are rewarded for being the first to arrive and the last to leave. The unwritten rule is that more hours equate to more dedication and, therefore, more success. However, this mindset can turn toxic. Companies set unrealistic benchmarks, making it nearly impossible to meet expectations without sacrificing personal well-being. The pressure to overwork doesn't necessarily lead to better results; it often leads to burnout and diminishing returns. Take, for instance, a corporate employee who constantly works overtime to meet "ambitious" goals. Initially, this might lead to praise and recognition. However, over time, the constant stress and lack of work-life balance decrease productivity and personal dissatisfaction. The employee starts to feel trapped in a cycle where no amount of effort seems sufficient, leading to chronic stress and burnout.

So, how can you tell when your ambition has slipped into perfectionism? There are several indicators. One of the most telling signs is never being satisfied with your achievements. No matter how well you perform, it never quite feels satisfying. You might finish a project only to immediately start worrying about the next one, unable to take a moment to celebrate your success. Chronic stress is another sign. If you find yourself constantly anxious about meeting expectations, it's a red flag. Burnout is the final, glaring indicator. When you're perpetually exhausted and emotionally drained, it's a clear sign that your drive for perfection is taking a toll on your well-being.

Maintaining healthy ambition involves setting realistic goals and embracing a growth mindset. Start by breaking larger goals into manageable tasks to make them feel less daunting. Prioritize progress over perfection. This shift in mindset can make a significant difference. Embrace a growth mindset, which values learning and development over flawless performance. Acknowledge that mistakes and setbacks are part of the learning process. They're not indications of failure but growth opportunities. Remember that it's okay to ask for help. Collaboration can lead to better outcomes and takes some of the pressure off you. Lastly, prioritize self-care. Ensure you're taking time to recharge. This not only improves your well-being but also boosts your productivity and creativity.

In sum, it's vital to recognize the difference between ambition and perfectionism. Ambition drives you forward, while perfectionism holds you back with fear and self-doubt. By setting realistic goals, celebrating progress, and prioritizing self-care, you can maintain healthy ambition and avoid the pitfalls of perfectionism.

1.4 Perfectionism vs. Excellence: Identifying Key Differences

Perfectionism and excellence might seem like two sides of the same coin, but they are fundamentally different. Excellence is about striving for greatness with flexibility and resilience. It's having high standards but also recognizing that mistakes are part of the process. Perfectionism, on the other hand, is rigid and unforgiving, demanding flawlessness and leading to a cycle of self-criticism and dissatisfaction.

To counteract these negative effects, self-compassion plays a crucial role in striving for excellence. When you're compassionate with yourself, you acknowledge your mistakes as normal parts of growth. You understand that errors don't define you but are opportunities to learn and improve. Perfectionism refuses that grace. It views any misstep as a failure, driving a harsh inner dialogue that can be mentally draining. Embracing self-compassion builds resilience, enabling you to bounce back from setbacks instead of getting stuck in fear.

The outcomes of pursuing excellence versus perfectionism are starkly different. Striving for excellence leads to sustainable success and well-being: you celebrate achievements, learn from mistakes, and maintain a healthy balance in life. In contrast, perfectionism often creates chronic dissatisfaction—nothing ever feels like enough. This endless self-criticism can trigger anxiety, depression, and risk aversion, making you afraid to take on new challenges. It can also lead to conditions like obsessive-compulsive disorder (OCD) and eating disorders, as the relentless pursuit of perfection can manifest in these harmful ways.

Consider the world of sports. An athlete focused on excellence hones skills incrementally, celebrates personal bests, and learns from losses. They see setbacks as part of the journey. However, an athlete with perfectionist tendencies might be debilitated by a single poor performance and unable to appreciate overall progress, risking burnout. The same pattern appears in business, where a leader aiming for excellence fosters innovation and growth, while a perfectionist leader stifles creativity through fear of mistakes.

Likewise, in the arts, a musician who pursues excellence embraces the creative process—even the imperfections. Meanwhile, a perfectionist musician becomes consumed by playing every note flawlessly, draining the joy from their craft.

Ultimately, excellence is about progress, learning, and resilience—upholding high standards with kindness toward yourself. Perfectionism, in its rigid and unforgiving form, can lead to a life of chronic dissatisfaction and mental health challenges. By choosing excellence and practicing self-compassion, you can achieve sustained success and well-being, and experience a sense of relief from the constant pressure of perfectionism.

1.5 The Role of Culture and Upbringing in Shaping Perfectionist Tendencies

Culture and upbringing play significant roles in shaping perfectionistic tendencies, often in ways that go unnoticed. Different cultures place varying degrees of emphasis on academic achievement, societal status, and public image, all of which can foster perfectionism. For instance, in many East Asian cultures, academic success is highly valued, and children are often under immense pressure to excel in school. This cultural emphasis on grades and performance can instill a belief that one's worth is tied to one's academic achievements. Educational systems prioritizing standardized testing and top-tier college admissions reinforce these pressures, making it easy to see how perfectionistic behaviors develop.

In Western cultures, societal status and public image can be equally influential. For example, the pressure to present a flawless image on social media has become a modern-day stressor. Platforms like Instagram and Facebook often showcase curated, seemingly perfect lives, making individuals feel inadequate and pushing them to strive for an unattainable ideal. The need to gain social approval through 'likes' and 'shares' can exacerbate perfectionistic tendencies, making people overly critical of themselves and constantly seeking validation.

Educational practices also contribute to perfectionism. Schools that reward only the highest achievers or impose punitive measures for mistakes can create an environment where students feel compelled to be perfect. The overemphasis on grades and standardized testing can make learning feel like a high-stakes competition rather than an enriching experience. This environment can stifle creativity and discourage risk-taking, as students focus more on avoiding mistakes than exploring new ideas.

Parental expectations significantly impact the development of perfectionism. Parents who place high demands on their children, whether academically, athletically, or socially, can inadvertently foster perfectionistic tendencies. When parents tie their approval and love to their child's achievements, it sends a message that being perfect is the only way to be valued. This can start at a very young age and become deeply ingrained. For instance, a child who receives praise solely for getting straight A's may internalize the belief that anything less than perfect is unacceptable. This mindset can lead to chronic self-criticism and a fear of failure that persists into adulthood.

The impact of familial expectations isn't always about overt pressure. Sometimes, it's the unspoken expectations or the modeling of perfectionistic behaviors by parents. A child who sees their parents constantly striving for perfection, never admitting mistakes, and fearing failure is likely to adopt similar behaviors. The subtle cues, like a parent's dissatisfaction with their minor errors or the relentless pursuit of success, can teach children that imperfection is intolerable.

Understanding the influence of culture and upbringing on perfectionism is crucial for addressing it. Recognizing that these external pressures shape internal beliefs can help you see that your perfectionistic tendencies aren't just personal flaws but are influenced by the environment you grew up in. This awareness can be empowering, giving you the control to question and challenge these ingrained beliefs, and create space for more self-compassion and realistic expectations.

As you reflect on your own experiences, consider how cultural norms, educational practices, and familial expectations have shaped your perceptions of success and self-worth. Acknowledging these influences is the first step in reshaping your mindset and moving towards a healthier, more balanced approach to life. By understanding the roots of your perfectionism, you can begin to untangle yourself from these external pressures and cultivate a more compassionate, realistic view of yourself and your achievements, feeling enlightened and motivated in the process.

We've lifted the hood on perfectionism, seeing it for what it is—an often misunderstood blend of high standards and deep-seated fears. Let that understanding spark compassion for yourself and anyone who's ever felt trapped by the need to be flawless. Up next, you'll discover how these patterns play out in personal relationships, where high expectations and vulnerability collide.

Chapter 2

Perfectionism in Personal Relationships

I magine you're at dinner with your partner, but instead of enjoying the moment, your mind is racing about how the evening could be better. The napkins aren't perfectly folded, and the conversation isn't flowing as smoothly as you'd hoped. You find yourself nitpicking, not just about the dinner but also about your partner's behavior, interactions, and even your role in the relationship. This relentless pursuit of perfection can strain your romantic relationship, creating a rift that's hard to bridge.

2.1 When Perfectionism Meets Partnership: Navigating Romantic Relationships

Perfectionism in relationships often leads to unrealistic expectations and pressures that can be incredibly damaging. When you hold yourself and your partner to impossible standards, dissatisfaction and emotional strain become inevitable. You might find yourself constantly critiquing your partner's actions, focusing on minor flaws rather than appreciating their efforts. This can lead to frustration and conflict, as your partner may feel unappreciated and undervalued. Over time, this critical atmosphere can create emotional distance, making it difficult to maintain intimacy and connection.

One of the most important aspects of overcoming perfectionism in relationships is differentiating between genuine needs and unrealistic expectations. Needs are essential for your well-being and the health of the relationship, like mutual respect, trust, and emotional support. Unrealistic expectations, on the other hand, can often be inflated and unattainable, such as expecting your partner to always know what you're thinking or never to make mistakes. For instance, expecting your partner to always agree with you or never have a bad day can be unrealistic. Clarifying this distinction can significantly improve relationship dynamics by reducing misunderstandings and conflicts. It allows both partners to focus on what truly matters and let go of minor imperfections that don't impact the core of the relationship.

Communication challenges are common in relationships where perfectionism is at play. Perfectionists often struggle with expressing vulnerability, fearing that showing any sign of weakness will lead to rejection or criticism. This fear can hinder emotional intimacy, making sharing your true feelings and concerns difficult. You might find yourself bottling up emotions, leading to resentment and further misunderstandings. Overcoming these communication pitfalls requires a balance of assertiveness and empathy. Being able to assertively express your needs while being empathetic to your partner's feelings can foster a more open and understanding relationship.

ACTION BOX: Relationship Dialogue and Reflection

- Purpose: Encourage open communication about each partner's genuine needs and realistic expectations.

- Approach: Pick a calm time—perhaps during a walk or after dinner—then share one or two questions at a time.

1. "What do I need most from you right now, and why is it important?"

2. "How might perfectionist habits show up for us, and how can we handle them together?"

3. "What small gesture makes you feel heard or understood?"

Follow-Up: Write any useful insights or ideas in a shared notebook or note-taking app. Revisit them weekly to track how your communication is evolving.

Effective communication is crucial, and there are several strategies you can employ to improve it. First, practice active listening. This means fully engaging with what your partner is saying without interrupting or planning your response while they're speaking. For instance, you can nod to show you're listening, ask clarifying questions, and summarize what your partner said to ensure you understand. Reflecting back on what you hear can also show that you understand their perspective. Using "I" statements can help express your feelings without sounding accusatory, such as "I feel overwhelmed when..." rather than "You always...". This approach reduces defensiveness and promotes constructive dialogue. Additionally, setting aside regular time for open and honest conversations can prevent small issues from escalating into major conflicts.

Fostering acceptance and appreciation is another key component. Instead of focusing on what your partner does wrong, try to appreciate what they do right. Acknowledge their efforts and express gratitude for their positive qualities. Reducing the impulse to "fix" or change each other can strengthen the relationship. Understand that everyone has flaws and that these imperfections are part of what makes each person unique and lovable. By embracing this mindset, you can create a more harmonious and loving partnership.

Regular relationship check-ins are a practical way to maintain alignment on needs and expectations. These check-ins don't have to be formal or lengthy; even a casual conversation over coffee can suffice. The goal is to touch base regularly on how each of you is feeling and address any concerns before they become significant issues. This practice helps ensure that both partners feel heard and valued and allows for adjustments as necessary to keep the relationship healthy and balanced.

2.2 Perfectionism and Parenting: Strategies for Balance

Imagine you're helping your child with their homework. You hover over them, correcting every little mistake, insisting they redo the work until it's flawless. Your intentions are good—you want them to succeed and be their best—but this approach can set impossibly high standards for both you and your child. Perfectionism in parenting often manifests in over-controlling or overly critical behaviors. You might find yourself micromanaging their activities, from school projects to social interactions, to help them avoid the mistakes you fear. However, this can create an environment where your child feels constant pressure to meet unattainable expectations.

The impact of such perfectionistic parenting on children can be profound. Kids raised in this environment often experience heightened anxiety, low self-esteem, and a pervasive fear of failure. They might internalize the belief that their worth is tied to their achievements, leading to a constant need to perform perfectly.

This can stifle their creativity and willingness to take risks, as the fear of making mistakes becomes paralyzing. Over time, these children may develop their own perfectionistic tendencies, mirroring the behaviors they observe. The stress of trying to live up to these high expectations can also lead to physical symptoms like headaches and stomachaches, as well as emotional issues such as depression and social withdrawal.

To counteract these negative effects, adopting a more balanced approach to parenting is crucial. This involves being flexible and forgiving, both with your child and yourself. Encourage effort and growth rather than perfection. Praise your child for their hard work, perseverance, and improvements rather than just the final outcome. Celebrate their attempts to foster a growth mindset even when they don't succeed. This approach helps them understand that mistakes are part of learning and growing, reducing their fear of failure. Model this behavior by showing them how you handle your mistakes with grace and a sense of humor, reinforcing that it's okay to be imperfect.

Promoting self-awareness in parents is also key. Take time to reflect on your perfectionist tendencies and how they might influence your parenting style. Are you setting standards that are too high, both for yourself and your child? Consider the example you're setting regarding handling mistakes and imperfections. Children learn a lot by observing their parents. If they see you being harsh on yourself for minor errors, they will likely adopt a similar attitude. By demonstrating self-compassion and a realistic approach to your own imperfections, you can teach your child to do the same.

ACTION BOX: Parenting Self-Awareness Journal

- Goal: Track moments when you feel compelled to micromanage or criticize your child's actions.

Method :
1. Briefly note the situation (e.g., "Homework time," "Playdate," "Mealtime").

2. Write down why you felt the urge to correct them: Was it fear of mistakes? Worry they'd fail?

3. Reflect on alternative responses: Could you have offered guidance without taking over?

Tip: Review your notes weekly and celebrate any instances where you gave your child more room to learn and grow at their own pace.

Creating a supportive and nurturing environment is essential for balanced parenting. Encourage open communication with your child, making it clear that they can come to you with their successes and struggles without fear of judgment. This builds trust and helps your child feel secure in sharing their experiences with you. Involve them in setting realistic goals and expectations, fostering a sense of autonomy and responsibility. This collaborative approach not only reduces pressure but also empowers your child to take ownership of their actions and learn from their experiences.

It's important to set boundaries for yourself as well. Recognize that you don't have to be the perfect parent. Allow yourself to make mistakes and learn from them. Seek support from other parents, parenting groups, or professionals if you feel overwhelmed. Remember, parenting is a continuous learning process, and striving for perfection can rob you of the joy and fulfillment that comes from connecting with your child and watching them grow. By embracing a balanced approach, you can create a positive and nurturing environment that promotes both your child's and your own well-being.

2.3 Building Friendships with Self-Compassion, Not Criticism

Imagine yourself with a group of friends, sharing stories and laughter. But instead of joining in the fun, you find yourself silently critiquing every word you say, every gesture you make. You worry about coming off as less than perfect, and this constant self-criticism makes it hard to truly connect with others. But what if you could be kinder to yourself? Practicing self-compassion can make a world of difference in your friendships. When you're kinder to yourself, you naturally become less judgmental of others. This shift can deepen your relationships, transforming them into more supportive and nurturing connections. Self-compassion reduces the inner critic that often spills over into how you interact with friends, making you a more understanding and empathetic companion.

Embracing imperfections in friendships is another crucial step. We often hold our friends to high standards, expecting them to be perfect in every way. But this expectation can strain relationships. Real friendships aren't about finding perfect people; they're about accepting and loving each other, flaws and all. Imagine a friend who always shows up late. Instead of focusing on their tardiness, try to appreciate their effort to be there for you, even if it's not always on time. Accepting these imperfections can actually strengthen your bond. It shows that you value the person for who they are, not just for how well they meet your expectations.

Promoting vulnerability and openness is a key to building stronger, more authentic friendships. Sharing your personal struggles and imperfections can create a sense of empathy and mutual understanding. This doesn't mean you have to reveal your deepest secrets at every opportunity, but being honest about your challenges can help your friends feel more connected to you. For instance, admitting that you're feeling overwhelmed at work or that you're dealing with a personal issue can invite your friends to support you. It also encourages them to share their own struggles, fostering a deeper connection. Vulnerability isn't a sign of weakness; it's a pathway to genuine intimacy.

Friendship Reflection Exercise

Take a moment to reflect on your friendships. Consider the following questions and write down your thoughts:

- How often do you critique your actions or words when you're with friends?

- What imperfections do you notice in your friends, and how do you react to them?

- Have you shared any personal struggles or vulnerabilities with your friends recently? How did they respond?

Use these reflections to guide your interactions, aiming to be more self-compassionate, accepting, and open.

Creating friendships based on self-compassion rather than criticism involves a conscious effort to change how you interact with yourself and others. It starts with recognizing your own worth and extending that same kindness to your friends. When you stop expecting perfection from yourself, you naturally stop expecting it from others. This doesn't mean lowering your standards or ignoring your values; it means understanding that everyone, including you, is a work in progress.

Imagine a friend who always seems to have their life together. They're successful at work, have a great social life, and always seem happy. It's easy to compare yourself to them and feel inadequate. But by practicing self-compassion, you can appreciate your journey and recognize that your friend has their own struggles, even if they're not visible. This shift in perspective allows you to support your friend without feeling envious or critical.

In a world where social media often showcases only the highlights of people's lives, it's important to remember that genuine relationships are built on authenticity and trust. Being open about your flaws and struggles can break the illusion of perfection and create a space where genuine connections can flourish. When you and your friends can laugh at your mistakes and support each other through tough times, your relationships become more resilient and meaningful.

So, the next time you're with friends, try to be mindful of your inner dialogue. Replace self-criticism with self-compassion. Embrace the imperfections that make each of you unique. Share your struggles and listen to theirs. These small changes can lead to deeper, more fulfilling friendships where everyone feels accepted and valued for who they are.

2.4 Setting Boundaries with Family to Foster Healthy Interactions

Picture yourself at a family gathering. The conversation turns critical, and before you know it, you're knee-deep in a discussion, leaving you emotionally drained. Setting healthy boundaries in such moments is crucial, especially when dealing with critical or demanding family members. Boundaries act as barriers that protect your mental health and personal values, allowing you to maintain a sense of self without being overwhelmed by familial expectations. They help you preserve your well-being, ensuring you don't lose yourself in the process of meeting others' demands.

Clear communication is key to setting and maintaining these boundaries. Start by identifying what you need to feel safe and respected in your interactions. This could be as simple as deciding you won't engage in conversations that make you uncomfortable or setting limits on how much time you spend with certain family members. When communicating these boundaries, be straightforward yet compassionate. Use "I" statements to express your needs without sounding accusatory, such as "I feel overwhelmed when we discuss politics. Can we talk about something else?" This approach minimizes defensiveness and fosters understanding.

Setting boundaries with close relatives can be particularly challenging. Parents and siblings may have known you your entire life and might resist changes in the dynamics. They might take it personally, feeling rejected or hurt. Navigating this requires sensitivity and patience. Acknowledge their feelings, but remain firm in your stance. You could say, "I understand this is new for you, but I need this boundary to take care of myself." It's also helpful to anticipate potential pushback and prepare responses that reinforce your boundaries without escalating the situation.

Finding a balance between meeting your needs and accommodating others' can lead to more fulfilling and less stressful relationships. Compromise plays a vital role here. While standing your ground is important, being too rigid can strain relationships. For example, if a family member constantly interrupts you, set a boundary by saying, "I appreciate your enthusiasm, but I need to finish my point before you respond." At the same time, be willing to listen and make adjustments where reasonable. This balance shows respect for both your needs and theirs, paving the way for healthier interactions.

Prioritizing self-care in family interactions is non-negotiable. Family obligations and expectations can be overwhelming, but maintaining your emotional and mental well-being should come first. This might mean taking breaks during family gatherings to recharge or limiting the frequency of visits if they become too taxing. Self-care isn't selfish; it's necessary. Taking care of yourself makes you better equipped to engage positively with your family. Incorporate practices that help you relax and stay grounded, such as deep breathing, meditation, or even a short walk.

Remember, setting boundaries is a process, not a one-time event. It requires ongoing effort and reinforcement. There will be times when your boundaries are tested, and it's essential to stay consistent. Reiterate your needs calmly and clearly, and stick to the consequences if your boundaries are crossed. Over time, your family will start to understand and respect your limits, even if it takes a while for them to adjust.

In summary, setting boundaries with family members is crucial for managing perfectionism and maintaining your well-being. Clear communication, sensitivity, and a willingness to compromise can help you navigate this challenging task. Prioritizing self-care ensures that you remain emotionally and mentally resilient, allowing you to engage with your family in a healthier, more balanced way. As you implement these boundaries, you'll notice a positive shift in your interactions and overall family dynamics, leading to more harmonious and fulfilling relationships.

Having explored how perfectionism can both magnify our best qualities and expose hidden insecurities in close relationships—and how empathy can ease its grip—we now turn to its impact in the workplace. Next, we'll look at ways to balance ambition with self-care so you can succeed without burning out.

Chapter 3

The Professional Perfectionist

I magine sitting in a job interview, your heart racing as you mentally review every detail of your resume and qualifications. The interviewer asks about your career goals, and you find yourself describing an ambitious path filled with prestigious roles and high-stakes projects. This vision sounds impressive, but deep down, you feel a gnawing uncertainty. Are you pursuing these goals because they align with your true passions, or are you driven by a need to meet external expectations and avoid the sting of perceived failure?

3.1 Perfectionism and Career Choices: A Double-Edged Sword

Perfectionism can significantly impact your career path, often steering you toward high-stress roles that promise prestige but come with the risk of burnout. If you're a perfectionist, you might gravitate towards careers that demand impeccable performance and constant validation. Think of fields like law, medicine, or finance, where the stakes are high and the margin for error is slim. These careers offer the allure of success and recognition, but they also come with immense pressure and long hours. The drive to be perfect can push you to work tirelessly, often at the expense of your mental and physical health. Over time, the relentless pursuit of perfection can lead to burnout, where exhaustion and stress overshadow any sense of accomplishment.

There's often a mismatch between personal values and professional roles for perfectionists. You might choose a career based on what you think you should do rather than what truly excites and fulfills you. This disconnect can lead to dissatisfaction and a lack of fulfillment as you find yourself in roles that clash with your core values. For example, you might pursue a high-paying corporate job because it's seen as a mark of success, even if your passion lies in a more creative or service-oriented field. The pressure to meet societal expectations can cloud your judgment, making it difficult to distinguish between what you want and what you think you need to achieve to be deemed successful.

To align your career choices with your personal values, start by evaluating what truly matters to you. Reflect on your strengths, interests, and the aspects of work that bring you joy and satisfaction. Consider what a fulfilling career looks like for you beyond the external markers of success. It might be helpful to write down your values and compare them with your current or prospective job roles. Are there discrepancies? If so, think about how you can bridge the gap. Maybe it's about finding a role that offers more creative freedom or allows you to positively impact your community. Aligning your career with your values can lead to greater satisfaction and a sense of purpose, reducing the need to chase perfection. This process of alignment is not just about finding a job; it's about taking control of your professional life and shaping it in a way that resonates with your true self.

Flexibility in career planning is another essential aspect. Embracing adaptability allows for growth, change, and learning from experiences rather than rigidly adhering to a flawed perception of the "ideal" career path. Understand that your career doesn't have to follow a linear trajectory. It's okay to pivot, take risks, and explore different opportunities. This flexibility can open doors to new experiences and perspectives, helping you discover passions and strengths you might not have realized. It also helps you stay resilient despite setbacks, as you're more willing to adjust your plans and learn from challenges. Embracing this flexibility can be a breath of fresh air, liberating you from the suffocating grip of perfectionism.

A practical exercise to help you align your career with your values is to create a Career Values Inventory. Write down what you value most in a job—whether it's creativity, autonomy, work-life balance, or contributing to society. Then, rate your current job or prospective roles based on how well they align with these values. This can provide clarity and guide your career decisions, ensuring they reflect your true aspirations rather than perfectionist ideals.

In the end, while perfectionism might drive you towards impressive career achievements, it's crucial to balance this drive with personal fulfillment and well-being. By aligning your career choices with your values and embracing flexibility, you can create a successful, satisfying, and sustainable professional life. This balance allows you to pursue excellence without the crippling pressure of perfectionism, leading to a healthier and more rewarding career.

3.2 Managing Perfectionism in Leadership and Team Dynamics

Imagine you're leading a team, and you can't help but set sky-high standards for every project. You want everything to be flawless, from the presentations to the tiniest details in reports. What you might not realize is that this perfectionism can have a ripple effect, inadvertently setting unrealistic expectations that strain your team's morale and productivity. When team members constantly feel they must meet impossible standards, stress levels rise, and efficiency drops. They might find themselves working late hours to meet these expectations, which can lead to burnout and resentment. The constant pressure can stifle creativity, as the fear of making mistakes overshadows the willingness to take risks and innovate.

Adopt realistic goals that encourage collaboration without perfectionist pressures. Break large projects into clear milestones to maintain motivation and clarity. Encourage open dialogue about these goals, inviting input from your team to ensure that everyone feels they are realistic and fair. This collaborative approach fosters a sense of ownership and motivation, as team members feel their voices are heard and valued.

Fostering a culture of growth and development is another key aspect. Shift the focus from flawless performance to continuous learning and improvement. Encourage your team to view challenges and setbacks as opportunities for growth rather than failures. Promote an environment where experimentation and innovation are valued, even if they come with occasional mistakes. This mindset helps build a resilient and innovative team that is not afraid to take calculated risks and learn from their experiences. Provide opportunities for professional development, such as workshops, training sessions, and mentorship programs. This enhances skills and reinforces the idea that growth and development are ongoing processes.

One of the most effective ways to support your team is through constructive feedback. The way you provide feedback can significantly impact your team's motivation and performance. Aim to give feedback that is specific, actionable, and focused on improvement rather than criticism. Start with positive observations to acknowledge what your team members are doing well, then provide constructive suggestions for areas of improvement. For example, instead of saying, "This report is not up to standard," you might say, "You did a great job on the research; however, adding more detailed analysis in this section could make it even stronger." This approach helps team members understand that their efforts are recognized and that feedback is aimed at assisting them to grow.

Feedback Reflection Exercise

Take a moment to reflect on your recent feedback experiences. Consider the following questions and write down your thoughts:

- How do you usually provide feedback to your team?

- What reactions do you notice from your team members when receiving feedback?

- How can you incorporate more positive observations into your feedback?

Use these reflections to guide your approach, aiming to provide feedback that motivates and educates.

Adopting these strategies can transform how your team operates, creating an environment where individuals feel supported and motivated to do their best work. It's also important to lead by example. Show your team that you value growth and learning by being open about your mistakes and what you've learned from them. This vulnerability can build trust and encourage your team to adopt a similar mindset. By modeling a balanced approach to leadership that prioritizes realistic goals, continuous development, and constructive feedback, you can help your team thrive without the burden of perfectionism.

Ultimately, managing perfectionism in leadership and team dynamics is about creating a supportive environment where individuals feel empowered to contribute their best work. By setting clear, achievable goals, fostering a culture of growth, and providing constructive feedback, you can build a resilient and innovative team that excels without the crippling pressure of perfectionism.

3.3 Strategies for Handling Criticism and Feedback at Work

Imagine sitting at your desk, an email notification pops up, and you see it's from your boss. Your heart sinks as you read through the feedback on your recent project. It's not all praise—there are pointed criticisms and suggestions for improvement. Feeling the sting of criticism is natural, but it's important to understand that feedback is a normal part of professional growth. It's not a personal attack but a tool to help you develop your skills and advance in your career. Normalizing the experience of receiving criticism can ease the emotional impact and help you view it as a constructive part of your professional journey.

Managing emotional responses to criticism can be challenging, but some techniques can help. When you first receive critical feedback, your immediate reaction might be defensiveness or anxiety. Try taking a few deep breaths to calm yourself. This simple act can help slow your heart rate and give you a moment to collect your thoughts. Another useful technique is reframing. Instead of seeing the feedback as a personal failure, view it as an opportunity to grow. Ask yourself, "What can I learn from this?" or "How can this help me improve?" Shifting your perspective from one of defeat to one of growth can significantly reduce the emotional impact of criticism.

Developing a growth mindset is crucial in handling feedback effectively. A growth mindset, a concept popularized by psychologist Carol Dweck, is the belief that abilities and intelligence can be developed through dedication and hard work. When you adopt this mindset, you see feedback as a valuable resource for learning and improvement rather than a judgment of your competence. To cultivate a growth mindset, remind yourself that skills and abilities are not fixed traits; they can be honed over time. Embrace challenges and view setbacks as part of the learning process. This approach will make you more resilient and open to feedback, enhancing your professional development.

Proactively seeking constructive feedback is another key strategy. Don't wait for your annual performance review to determine how you're doing. Regularly ask for specific, actionable feedback from your peers and supervisors. When soliciting feedback, be clear about what you need. Instead of asking, "How did I do?" try asking, "Can you provide feedback on how I handled the client presentation?" or "What specific areas can I improve in my report writing?" This specificity encourages more valuable and detailed responses. It also shows that you are committed to your growth and open to learning, which can positively influence how others perceive you.

Feedback Request Template

Create a template for requesting feedback to make the process more straightforward. Here's an example you can use and modify:

Subject: Request for Feedback on [Specific Task/Project]

Dear [Name],

I hope this message finds you well. I'm reaching out to request your feedback on [specific task/project]. I'm particularly interested in understanding [specific aspect, e.g., "how I handled the client presentation," "the clarity and structure of my report," "my approach to team collaboration"]. Your insights would be incredibly valuable for my professional growth.

Thank you for your time and assistance.

Best regards, [Your Name]

Use this template to seek targeted feedback that can help you improve specific areas of your work.

Remember, feedback is not just about receiving; it's also about how you respond. Show appreciation for the input, even if it's hard to hear. A simple "Thank you for your feedback; I appreciate your insights" can go a long way in demonstrating professionalism and openness. If the feedback is unclear, don't hesitate to ask for clarification. Phrases like "Could you provide an example of what you mean?" or "Can you suggest ways I can improve in this area?" show that you're genuinely interested in understanding and acting on the feedback.

Integrating these strategies into your professional life can transform how you perceive and handle criticism. By normalizing feedback, managing your emotional responses, adopting a growth mindset, and proactively seeking constructive input, you'll become more resilient, skilled, and confident in your abilities. This balanced approach will help you thrive in your career without the paralyzing fear of imperfection.

3.4 Achieving Balanced Productivity: Tools for Professionals

Ever find yourself stuck in the endless loop of tweaking a report, trying to make it flawless, only to realize hours have slipped by? The myth of perfect work can be a major productivity killer. Striving for perfection often leads to paralysis by analysis, where you spend so much time refining and re-refining that you end up missing deadlines or exhausting yourself. Instead, embrace the concept of "good enough". This doesn't mean you're settling for mediocrity; instead, it's about setting realistic goals that prioritize quality without the unrealistic pressure of perfectionism. By aiming for the "this will do for now" standard, you free up mental space and time for other important tasks, maintaining a healthy balance between high standards and efficiency.

Setting healthy professional boundaries is crucial for maintaining both productivity and well-being. In today's connected world, it's easy to blur the lines between work and personal life. You might find yourself answering emails late at night or working through weekends, thinking you're being productive. But this constant connectivity can lead to burnout. Establish precise work hours and stick to them. Use tools like calendar apps to block out time for focused work and personal activities. Communicate your boundaries to colleagues and supervisors, letting them know when you're available and when you're not. This might initially feel uncomfortable, but it's essential for protecting your time and preventing work from encroaching on your personal life. This empowerment of setting boundaries can make you feel more in control of your time and well-being.

Work-life integration, rather than strict separation, can also help maintain productivity and mental health. Flexible working arrangements, such as remote work or adjustable hours, allow you to blend work tasks with personal responsibilities more seamlessly. This integration helps reduce the stress of juggling multiple roles and can lead to a more balanced and fulfilling life. Structured breaks and downtime are equally important. Incorporate short breaks throughout your day to recharge. This could be anything from a quick walk around the block to a few minutes of deep breathing exercises. These breaks can boost your focus, creativity, and overall well-being, making you more productive in the long run.

Regular self-assessment is another key tool for achieving balanced productivity. Take time to reflect on your professional ambitions and ensure they align with your personal values and well-being. This self-assessment can help you identify areas where perfectionism might be driving you toward unrealistic goals or unhealthy work habits. Use tools like journaling or self-reflection exercises to regularly check in with yourself. Ask questions like, "Are my current goals aligned with my values?" or "Am I maintaining a healthy balance between work and personal life?" These reflections can provide valuable insights and help you make necessary adjustments to stay on track.

Professional support services can also play a vital role in managing stress and maintaining a healthy work-life balance. Counseling services, wellness programs, and employee assistance programs offer resources and support to help you navigate the challenges of perfectionism. Don't hesitate to seek out these services if you're feeling overwhelmed. They can provide strategies for managing stress, improving mental health, and enhancing overall well-being. Joining a support group or finding a mentor can also offer guidance and encouragement, helping you stay grounded and focused on what truly matters.

Incorporating these strategies into your professional life can help you achieve balanced productivity without the crippling weight of perfectionism. This balance allows you to excel in your career without sacrificing personal happiness and fulfillment.

As you navigate the complexities of professional life, remember that achieving balance is a continuous process. It requires ongoing effort and adjustment, but the rewards are well worth it. By implementing these tools and strategies, you can create a more sustainable and satisfying professional life free from the relentless pressure of perfectionism.

Here, we explored how perfectionism impacts ambition, leadership and how we handle feedback. Real success comes not from rigid standards but from balancing drive with self-care and collaboration. Now, we'll widen the lens to watch perfectionism evolve over the different stages of life, from school days to retirement.

Chapter 4

Perfectionism's Impact Across Life's Stages

I magine a young girl meticulously arranging her collection of stuffed animals before bed. Every bear, bunny, and doll must be in its proper place and aligned perfectly. If even one is out of order, she can't sleep. This behavior might seem innocuous or even endearing at first glance. However, it can be an early sign of perfectionism. This trait can grow and intensify over time, impacting various stages of life. Perfectionism doesn't just appear overnight; it often begins in childhood and evolves as we age, shaped by our experiences and the expectations placed upon us.

4.1 Growing Up with Perfectionism: From Childhood to Adolescence

Recognizing early signs of perfectionism is crucial for intervening before it becomes pervasive. Perfectionism can manifest in various ways in children. They might have trouble completing assignments because they are never satisfied with their work. They may exhibit intense anxiety about making mistakes or facing criticism, leading to procrastination and avoidance behaviors. You might notice a child who is overly critical of themselves and others, showing extreme frustration over minor errors. These behaviors are more than just quirks; they are red flags that can indicate the onset of perfectionism.

The role of parents, teachers, and educational systems in fostering or mitigating these tendencies is significant. A child who grows up in an environment where high standards are emphasized without room for mistakes may internalize the belief that their worth is tied to their achievements. Controlling parenting styles, where children are constantly pushed to excel, can exacerbate perfectionist tendencies. Schools that emphasize grades and standardized testing over the learning process can also contribute. On the flip side, environments that celebrate effort, growth, and learning from mistakes can help mitigate perfectionistic tendencies. Encouraging children to embrace challenges and view setbacks as opportunities for growth can foster a healthier approach to achievement.

As children transition to adolescence, perfectionism often intensifies. Adolescence is a period of significant physical, emotional, and social changes. Teenagers face increased academic expectations, peer pressure, and societal standards, all of which can exacerbate perfectionistic tendencies. The early indicators observed in childhood, such as fear of failure and self-criticism, can evolve into more pronounced behaviors. Adolescents might become overly focused on their grades, engaging in unhealthy study habits and experiencing high levels of stress and anxiety. Social media comparisons amplify these pressures, as teens strive to present a perfect image to their peers, often leading to feelings of inadequacy and low self-esteem.

The unique pressures that teenagers encounter can build upon the foundation laid during childhood. Academic expectations are a significant source of stress. The competition for college admissions and the pressure to excel can drive teens to set unrealistic standards for themselves. Peer relationships also play a crucial role. Adolescents are acutely aware of their social standing. They might go to great lengths to fit in, fearing rejection if they don't meet certain standards. Societal standards, perpetuated by media and cultural norms, add another layer of pressure, pushing teens to conform to idealized images of success and beauty. These compounded pressures can make the adolescent years particularly challenging for those with perfectionist tendencies.

Parents and educators can implement several strategies to support children and adolescents in developing healthy ambition. Fostering resilience and self-acceptance is key. Celebrate effort and progress rather than just outcomes. Encourage children to set realistic goals and to view mistakes as learning opportunities. Teach them to manage academic stress by breaking tasks into manageable steps and prioritizing self-care. Provide a supportive environment where they feel safe to express their fears and challenges. For adolescents, helping them navigate social dynamics is crucial. Encourage open communication about the pressures they face and offer guidance on building healthy, supportive relationships.

Reflection Section

Take a moment to reflect on your experiences with perfectionism during childhood and adolescence. Consider the following questions and jot down your thoughts:

- What early signs of perfectionism did you notice in yourself or others?

- How did your parents, teachers, or school environment influence your perfectionist tendencies?

- What pressures did you face during adolescence, and how did they impact your behavior?

Use these reflections to better understand how your past experiences have shaped your perfectionism and to identify areas where you can make positive changes.

Incorporating these strategies and reflections can help children and adolescents develop a healthier relationship with achievement, reducing the risk of maladaptive perfectionism and promoting well-being.

4.2 The Perfectionist's Prime: Navigating Adulthood

You're in your late twenties or early thirties, and life feels like a high-wire act. Career advancement is crucial, and you're constantly juggling projects, meetings, and deadlines. You want to climb the corporate ladder, but the pressure to perform flawlessly can be overwhelming. The stakes are high; one mistake could mean losing a promotion or, worse, your job. This is a peak period for perfectionism to rear its head. The relentless pursuit of career success can lead to burnout as you push yourself to meet unrealistic expectations. You might find yourself working late hours, sacrificing personal time, and feeling a constant undercurrent of stress.

Relationships add another layer of complexity. Whether you're dating, married, or somewhere in between, the pressure to be the perfect partner can be immense. You want to be supportive, attentive, and loving, but perfectionism can make you hyper-aware of your flaws and those of your partner. This hyperawareness can lead to feelings of inadequacy and dissatisfaction, making it challenging to maintain a healthy, balanced relationship. You might be overanalyzing interactions, fearing any misstep will jeopardize your relationship. The emotional toll can be significant as you struggle to meet both your and your partner's expectations.

Personal development is also a significant focus during this stage of life. You're trying to figure out who you are, what you want, and how to get there. The desire for self-improvement is strong, but perfectionism can turn this into a never-ending quest for an unattainable ideal. You may set lofty goals for yourself, only to feel crushed when you inevitably fall short. This can lead to a cycle of self-criticism and frustration, making it difficult to appreciate your progress and achievements. The constant drive to be better can overshadow the joy of personal growth, leaving you feeling perpetually unsatisfied.

Balancing these pressures requires a mindful approach. Managing perfectionism while pursuing personal and professional goals involves recognizing your limits and setting realistic expectations. Start by acknowledging that you can't do everything perfectly, and that's okay. Focus on what truly matters and prioritize tasks that align with your values and goals. Delegate when possible, and don't be afraid to ask for help. This can free up time and mental energy, allowing you to focus on high-impact activities without spreading yourself too thin.

Work-life balance is crucial. Establish boundaries between your professional and personal life to prevent burnout. Set specific work hours and stick to them. Use tools like calendars and task management apps to organize your time effectively. Schedule regular breaks throughout your day to recharge. These breaks can be as simple as a short walk, a few minutes of deep breathing, or a quick chat with a friend. Prioritizing self-care is essential. Make time for activities that nourish your body and mind, such as exercise, hobbies, and spending time with loved ones. These activities can help you relax and recharge, making you more resilient to the pressures of perfectionism.

Mindfulness practices can also be beneficial. Techniques like meditation and mindful breathing can help you stay present and reduce stress. These practices can ground you, making it easier to manage the pressures of perfectionism. Reflect on your accomplishments and celebrate small victories. This can help shift your focus from what you haven't achieved to what you have, fostering a sense of gratitude and satisfaction. Remember that personal and professional growth is a journey, not a destination. Embrace imperfections as part of the process and recognize that they contribute to your unique path.

4.3 Midlife Reckoning: Perfectionism and the Search for Meaning

In the middle of your life, you might find yourself stopping to take stock of everything you've achieved and everything you haven't. This period, often called a midlife crisis or midlife reckoning, prompts a profound reevaluation of personal and professional accomplishments. You might begin to question the paths you've taken, the choices you've made, and the goals you've set. This introspection can intensify perfectionist tendencies as you scrutinize your past decisions and current status with a critical eye. The internal dialogue might go something like, "Have I done enough? Have I been perfect enough?" These questions can lead to a heightened sense of urgency to perfect areas of life that feel incomplete or unsatisfactory, often resulting in increased stress and anxiety.

The search for meaning beyond perfection becomes a central theme during this stage. It's no longer just about achieving career milestones or hitting personal benchmarks. Instead, you start to seek deeper fulfillment from passions, hobbies, and relationships that resonate with your core values. You might find joy in pursuits that have nothing to do with external validation, like painting, gardening, or volunteering. These activities offer a sense of purpose that transcends the superficial markers of success. In relationships, you may begin to prioritize genuine connections over appearances, valuing emotional intimacy and mutual support over the facade of a perfect partnership. This shift in focus helps to counterbalance the perfectionist tendencies, offering a more holistic and fulfilling approach to life.

Navigating life transitions such as career changes or retirement can further challenge your perfectionist mindset. These transitions often come with uncertainty and a loss of identity, which can trigger a desire to control every aspect of the new phase. You might feel the need to have a perfectly mapped-out plan for your career shift or an ideal vision of what retirement should look like. However, this approach can be paralyzing. Instead, embracing flexibility and being open to the unexpected can make these transitions smoother and less stressful. Allowing yourself to make mistakes and learn from them can transform these periods of change into opportunities for growth and self-discovery.

One practical way to manage these transitions without succumbing to perfectionistic pressures is to set realistic, flexible goals. Instead of fixating on an ideal outcome, focus on the process and be open to adjustments along the way. For instance, if you're considering a career change, start with small steps like networking with professionals in the field, taking relevant courses, or exploring new fields through volunteer work. These incremental actions can help you build confidence and gain clarity without the overwhelming pressure to achieve perfection immediately. Similarly, if you're transitioning into retirement, experiment with different activities and routines to find what truly brings you joy and fulfillment.

Another key strategy is to seek support from others who have navigated similar transitions. Mentors, friends, and support groups can offer valuable insights and encouragement, helping you to feel less isolated in your experiences. Sharing your fears and challenges with others can also provide relief as you realize that perfection is not a prerequisite for success or happiness. This sense of community can be a powerful antidote to the isolation and self-criticism that often accompany perfectionism, providing a sense of relief and connection.

Midlife is a time of profound change and reflection. By embracing a search for meaning beyond perfection and navigating transitions with flexibility and support, you can mitigate the intensifying perfectionist tendencies and find a deeper, more authentic sense of fulfillment.

4.4 Golden Years, Tarnished by Perfection? Elderly and Expectations

As you grow older, perfectionism can take on new forms and present unique challenges. Aging often brings physical changes that require adaptation, which can be particularly tough for perfectionists. You might find yourself grappling with the frustration of not being able to do things you once did effortlessly. Once simple tasks, like gardening or even getting up from a chair, may now require more effort. This can lead to feelings of inadequacy and a heightened sense of loss. The physical limitations imposed by aging can make you hyper-aware of your imperfections, and the desire to hide or deny these changes can be intense.

Shifting social roles also plays a significant part. Retirement, for instance, can be a double-edged sword. On one hand, it offers the freedom to pursue hobbies and interests. On the other, it can strip away a significant part of your identity, especially if you were someone who drew a lot of self-worth from your career. This loss can amplify perfectionist tendencies, as you might feel the need to prove your value in other ways. Social roles evolve, and the once-clear definitions of your contributions become blurry, making it difficult to find a new sense of purpose. You might start to overcompensate in other areas, like becoming overly meticulous about household tasks or focusing intensely on your appearance.

However, with age comes wisdom, which can be a powerful tool in mitigating perfectionism. The years bring with them a wealth of experiences and perspectives that can help you see the bigger picture. You begin to understand that life is not about flawless performance but about meaningful connections and contributions. This wisdom allows you to focus on life satisfaction and legacy rather than day-to-day perfection. You might find yourself valuing the relationships you've built, the lives you've touched, and the memories you've created more than any material or superficial achievements. This shift in focus can be incredibly liberating, allowing you to let go of the need to be perfect and instead embrace the richness of your imperfect life.

Support systems become increasingly important as you navigate these changes. Social support, community engagement, and mental health resources can provide the emotional and practical assistance you need. Surrounding yourself with a supportive network of family and friends can help you feel less isolated in your struggles with perfectionism. Engaging in community activities, whether it's volunteering, joining clubs, or participating in local events, can offer a sense of belonging and purpose. These interactions can remind you that everyone has imperfections and that these imperfections do not diminish your worth.

Mental health resources, such as counseling or support groups, can also be invaluable. Speaking with a therapist who understands the nuances of perfectionism can provide you with strategies to manage your tendencies. Support groups offer a space to share your experiences and hear from others facing similar challenges. Knowing that you are not alone can be incredibly comforting. It can help you develop a more compassionate perspective towards yourself, reassuring you that there are resources and people who can help you navigate your journey.

As you navigate your golden years, remember that perfection is not the goal. Wisdom, perspective, and support systems can help you focus on what truly matters—life satisfaction and the legacy you leave behind. Embrace the imperfections that come with aging and allow yourself to enjoy the richness of your experiences. You have lived a life full of ups and downs, and this tapestry of experiences makes you uniquely valuable.

4.5 Life Transitions as Perfectionist Pitfalls: Navigating Major Changes

Picture the day you get married, a joyous occasion filled with love and celebration. Yet, behind the smiles and laughter, you might obsess over every tiny detail, from the flower arrangements to the seating chart. These significant life transitions, like marriage, parenthood, and career changes, often serve as triggers for perfectionistic tendencies. Marriage, for instance, can bring about the pressure to be the perfect spouse, maintaining an ideal relationship that meets both your expectations and those of society. As discussed earlier, navigating romantic relationships requires balancing high standards with realistic expectations, a principle that becomes even more critical during such transitions.

Parenthood is another major transition that can exacerbate perfectionistic behaviors. The desire to be the perfect parent can lead to over-controlling and excessively critical parenting styles. You might be micromanaging every aspect of your child's life, driven by the fear of making mistakes. This can create a stressful environment for both you and your child. Balancing ambition with well-being, as discussed in the context of parenting, is crucial here. Setting healthy boundaries and allowing room for flexibility can help mitigate the pressures of perfectionism.

Career changes, whether they involve a promotion, a new job, or a complete shift in career paths, can also trigger perfectionistic tendencies. The pressure to prove yourself in a new role or to meet the high expectations associated with a promotion can be overwhelming. As discussed in the section on career choices, aligning your professional goals with your personal values and setting realistic expectations are key strategies for managing these transitions. Recognizing that these changes are part of your professional growth and not a test of your worth can help you navigate them more effectively.

Understanding that life transitions can lead to either adaptive growth or maladaptive perfectionistic behaviors is essential. Adaptive responses involve embracing change with a flexible mindset, focusing on growth and learning. Maladaptive behaviors, on the other hand, are characterized by rigid standards and an inability to accept anything less than perfection. During these transitions, it's important to apply a few principles that can help you respond adaptively to the challenges and uncertainties that come with significant life changes.

Strategies for navigating these transitions involve practical tools and techniques. Practicing self-compassion is fundamental. Allow yourself to make mistakes and view them as learning opportunities rather than failures. This can reduce the pressure to be perfect and help you approach transitions with a more relaxed and open mindset. Setting realistic expectations is equally important. Break down your goals into manageable steps and celebrate small victories along the way. This can make the transition feel less daunting and more achievable.

Flexibility is another key strategy. Life transitions are often unpredictable, and being open to change can help you adapt more easily. Embrace the unknown and be willing to adjust your plans as needed. Reflect on your values and priorities, and let them guide you through the transition. This can provide a sense of direction and purpose, even when things don't go as planned.

These strategies offer practical tools for managing perfectionism during major life transitions, helping you navigate these changes with confidence and resilience. By applying the principles of self-compassion, realistic expectations, and flexibility, you can turn these potential pitfalls into opportunities for growth and personal development.

From childhood to the golden years, perfectionism morphs but rarely disappears, shaping how we learn, work, and adjust to life's changes. Knowing this evolution makes it easier to adapt strategies that fit each stage. As we move forward, we'll explore the tangible strategies and tools to help curb perfectionism in your daily life. These practical applications will provide a comprehensive toolkit to manage perfectionism across various aspects of your life.

Chapter 5

Mindset Shifts: From Fixed to Growth

Picture yourself at a crossroads with a colossal project looming over you. The thought of beginning feels suffocating because, in your mind, it must be perfect from the get-go. This relentless pressure isn't just about high standards; it's rooted in something more profound—a fixed mindset. But what if I told you there's a different approach? One where mistakes are not failures but stepping stones, and growth is celebrated over perfection. Welcome to the transformative world of the growth mindset.

5.1 Cultivating a Growth Mindset: The First Steps

Understanding the difference between a fixed and a growth mindset is crucial. A fixed mindset, as Carol Dweck explores in her research, is the belief that your qualities, like intelligence and talent, are static and unchangeable. You might have grown up hearing phrases like, "You're so smart" or "You have a natural talent." While these sound like compliments, they can lead to a fixed mindset where you feel the need to constantly prove yourself. In contrast, a growth mindset revolves around the belief that your abilities can develop through effort, learning, and perseverance. With this mindset, challenges are not threats but opportunities to grow.

Identifying triggers for a fixed mindset lays the groundwork for change. Common triggers include facing setbacks, receiving negative feedback, or even seeing others succeed. For instance, you might feel demoralized when a colleague gets praised for their work, thinking their success diminishes your worth. Or perhaps, when you encounter a challenging task, you might avoid it altogether, fearing that any effort will highlight your shortcomings. Recognizing these triggers is the first step in shifting from a fixed to a growth mindset.

Practical strategies for transitioning include challenging negative thoughts and reframing them positively. When you catch yourself thinking, "I'm not good at this," remind yourself that skills grow with practice. Reframing is the process of changing the way you view a situation. It's about looking at things from a different perspective, one that is more empowering and growth-oriented. For example, consider a mistake not as a failure but as a valuable feedback. Instead of feeling defeated by a poor performance review, view it as a detailed map showing you exactly where to improve.

ACTION BOX: Spotting Fixed Mindset Moments

- Why: Recognize when you slip into rigid thinking so you can pivot to a growth perspective.

Directions:

1. Each evening, jot down any event that made you feel "stuck," anxious, or inadequate.

2. Ask yourself: "Which of my beliefs triggered that response?"

3. Brainstorm at least one kinder or more constructive way to view that same situation.

Note: Consistency is key—daily check-ins reveal patterns and help you practice reframing day by day.

Remember, the prompts provided here are simply a starting point. Feel free to adjust the questions or the timing to match your daily routine and personal reflection style. There's no "one-size-fits-all" approach—what matters most is finding a method that works for you.

Celebrating effort is essential to fostering a growth mindset. Shift from outcomes to appreciating your dedication and learning process. Recognize your hard work regardless of immediate results. This positive internal dialogue builds self-support, significantly enhancing your self-perception and personal growth over time.

By understanding the difference between fixed and growth mindsets, identifying triggers, and actively practicing reframing and celebrating effort, you pave the way for a more resilient and fulfilling approach to life.

5.2 Perfectionism and Forgiveness: Letting Go of Past Mistakes

Perfectionism often creates a barrier to self-forgiveness, making it difficult to move past mistakes. Imagine you've made an error at work, something minor but enough to trigger a cascade of self-reproach. You replay the incident over and over, each time feeling the weight of guilt grow heavier. This inability to forgive yourself can lead to prolonged guilt and a harsh inner dialogue that fuels your perfectionist tendencies. Holding onto these feelings doesn't just affect your emotional well-being; it can also hinder your ability to take risks and grow.

Forgiveness plays a crucial role in mental health. When you forgive yourself, you release the emotional burden that comes with guilt and regret. This emotional release can lead to significant healing, reducing anxiety and improving your overall well-being. Self-forgiveness allows you to acknowledge your mistakes without letting them define you. It helps you see your worth beyond your flaws, fostering a healthier and more compassionate relationship with yourself. This process can be incredibly freeing, allowing you to move forward with a lighter heart and a clearer mind.

ACTION BOX: Forgiveness Writing & Visualization

- Purpose: Let go of guilt or regret tied to perfectionistic mistakes.

Reflective Writing:

    1. Choose a past mistake you can't shake off.

    2. Free-write about what happened, focusing on lessons learned rather than blame.

Visualization:

    1. Close your eyes and envision placing that guilt or regret into a "container."

    2. Picture it drifting away—allowing emotional relief as you accept your imperfections.

*Ongoing Practice: Revisit these techniques whenever self-criticism resurfaces.

Maintaining a forgiving mindset requires ongoing effort. One helpful approach is to incorporate daily affirmations into your routine. Start your day with statements like, "I forgive myself for my mistakes and embrace the lessons they bring." These affirmations are not just words, they are a support system that can reshape your inner dialogue, making it more supportive and compassionate. Another strategy is to practice mindfulness. When you notice guilt or self-criticism creeping in, take a moment to breathe deeply and ground yourself in the present.

Acknowledge these feelings without judgment and remind yourself that it's okay to be imperfect.

<u>Forgiveness Reflection Exercise</u>

Set aside a few minutes each day to reflect on moments where you felt guilt or self-criticism. Ask yourself:

- What mistake did I make today that I'm struggling to forgive?

- What lesson can I learn from this mistake?

- How can I show myself compassion in this moment?

Write down your reflections and revisit them regularly to track your progress.

These practices can help prevent the buildup of guilt and self-criticism that often fuels perfectionism. By consistently choosing to forgive yourself and embrace your imperfections, you create a more compassionate and resilient mindset. This shift alleviates the emotional burden of perfectionism and opens up space for growth and self-acceptance.

5.3 Self-Talk for the Perfectionist: Scripts for Growth

Imagine this: you've just finished a presentation at work. Instead of feeling relieved, your mind is filled with a relentless stream of criticism. "That slide was a mess," "I stumbled over my words," "Everyone must think I'm incompetent." This is the power of self-talk. For perfectionists, internal dialogue can be a harsh critic, impacting your mindset and actions. Negative self-talk reinforces a fixed mindset, making you believe that any mistake defines your worth. This internal monologue can be debilitating, affecting your confidence and willingness to take risks.

Transforming self-talk is crucial for shifting to a growth mindset. One effective strategy is to consciously replace negative thoughts with positive, growth-oriented narratives. When you catch yourself thinking, "I can't do this," try reframing it to, "I'm learning to do this." This subtle shift changes the focus from limitation to possibility. Another approach is to practice gratitude. Instead of fixating on what went wrong, acknowledge what went right and what you've learned. For example, after that imperfect presentation, tell yourself, "I did my best under pressure, and I learned how to improve for next time." This reframing helps build resilience and a more positive outlook.

To guide you, here are some specific scripts to use in moments of self-doubt or criticism. When you think, "I'm not good enough," replace it with, "I am capable and always improving." If you find yourself saying, "I failed," try, "I discovered a new way that doesn't work, and now I know better." These scripts might feel awkward at first, but with practice, they can become second nature. Another useful phrase is, "I'm proud of my effort," which shifts the focus from outcomes to the hard work you put in. This helps in recognizing and celebrating your efforts, fostering a growth-oriented mindset.

ACTION BOX: Self-Talk Reflection Journal

- Purpose: Track how your internal dialogue shifts from negative to positive, reinforcing a growth-minded approach.

Method:

1. At day's end, recall one specific instance where you caught yourself engaging in self-critical or perfectionist language ("I messed up everything," "I can never get this right").

2. Rewrite that statement using a kinder, more constructive tone ("I learned something important today," "I'm improving each time I practice").

3. Note how this rewording affected your emotions or motivation. Did it boost your confidence? Reduce anxiety?

Follow-Up: Review your notes weekly. Highlight which reframes felt most genuine or had the greatest impact, and continue practicing them in daily life.

Each exercise in this book is a suggestion, not a mandate. Feel free to modify the activity, the duration, or even the focus as needed. The most important part is that you're engaging in a practice that helps you move toward a more balanced and authentic self.

Regular practice is essential. Just like building any new skill, shifting your self-talk works best when you do it consistently. After filling out your Reflection Journal, spend a minute each evening acknowledging one thought you reframed. Use an affirmation—such as "I am a work in progress, and that's okay"—to prime your mind for growth. Over time, these daily check-ins will gradually replace the old, critical voice with one that's more supportive and encouraging, reinforcing the progress you're making toward healthier self-talk.

5.4 The Power of Yet: Embracing Progress over Perfection

Imagine you're struggling to learn a new skill, like playing the guitar. You might find yourself saying, "I can't play this song." Now, add one small but powerful word: "yet." Suddenly, "I can't play this song" transforms into "I can't play this song yet." This simple addition shifts your perspective from a fixed mindset to a growth mindset. Instead of feeling defeated by your current inability, you recognize that you're on a path of learning and improvement. The word "yet" opens up a world of possibilities, suggesting that with time, effort, and practice, you will get there.

Building resilience through the power of "yet" involves framing challenges as temporary setbacks rather than insurmountable obstacles. When faced with difficulties, this mindset shift helps you see them as part of the learning process. For instance, if you're working on a complex project at work and encounter a problem, saying, "I haven't figured this out yet," can be incredibly empowering. It reassures you that the solution is within reach and that persistence will pay off. This approach fosters resilience, as you become more willing to tackle challenges head-on, knowing that your current struggles are not permanent.

Applying the power of "yet" in daily life can transform various aspects of your existence. In your professional life, if you find yourself overwhelmed by a new task, remind yourself, "I don't understand this yet." This mindset encourages you to seek out resources, ask for help, and continue learning until you master the task. In personal development, perhaps you're trying to build healthier habits but keep falling short. Instead of saying, "I can't stick to my routine," try, "I haven't found the right routine yet." This keeps you motivated to experiment and find what works for you.

Even in learning new hobbies, the power of "yet" can be a game-changer. If you're learning to cook and your first few attempts are less than stellar, telling yourself, "I'm not a great cook yet," keeps you open to trying new recipes and techniques without getting discouraged. This mindset encourages a focus on progress and learning, rather than immediate perfection. It helps you celebrate small victories along the way, reinforcing the idea that growth is a continuous process.

Incorporating the power of "yet" into your self-talk can make a significant difference in how you approach challenges. It transforms your internal dialogue from one of limitation to one of possibility. This shift not only enhances your resilience but also boosts your confidence, making you more likely to take on new challenges and persist in the face of setbacks. The power of "yet" reminds you that growth and improvement are always possible, turning every challenge into an opportunity for development.

5.5 Perfectionism and Procrastination: The Fear of Failure and the Paralysis of Perfection

Imagine sitting at your desk, knowing you have a significant project to start. Still, every time you think about it, a wave of anxiety washes over you. This is the fear of failure, magnified in the perfectionist's psyche. The thought of not meeting your own high standards can be so overwhelming that it leads to avoidance. You might find yourself doing anything but the task—cleaning, checking emails, or scrolling through social media. This avoidance, driven by the fear of failure, can create a cycle of procrastination that is hard to break. Instead of diving into the project, you put it off, hoping that somehow the task will become easier or the perfect moment will arrive, which it rarely does.

The paralysis of perfection is a real and daunting experience. When you're a perfectionist, the fear of failing to achieve perfection can be crippling. This fear doesn't just slow you down; it can bring your projects to a complete standstill. You might have a brilliant idea for a presentation, but the anxiety over every detail being flawless can prevent you from even starting. This paralysis can manifest in various ways, from endless planning and over-researching to constantly second-guessing your decisions. The result is that you end up doing nothing, trapped in a cycle of inaction and self-doubt.

Reframing failure is a powerful tool in overcoming this paralysis. Instead of seeing failure as a negative endpoint, try viewing it as an essential step in your growth and learning process. Think about it: every mistake you make is a lesson learned, a piece of feedback that guides you towards improvement. Embracing this mindset can transform how you approach tasks. Rather than fearing the possibility of failure, you begin to see it as an opportunity to gain new insights and refine your skills. This shift in perspective can reduce the anxiety associated with starting new projects and help you move forward with more confidence and resilience.

Breaking the cycle of perfectionism-induced procrastination involves practical strategies that can make a significant difference in your productivity and well-being. One effective approach is setting realistic goals. Instead of aiming for perfection, set achievable targets that allow for progress and learning. This can help you focus on completing tasks rather than getting stuck in pursuing flawless results. Embracing a "enoughness" philosophy can also be liberating. Accept that not everything needs to be perfect and that doing your best is often more than sufficient. This mindset can alleviate the pressure to be perfect and encourage you to take action, even if the outcome isn't ideal.

Overcoming the inertia of perfectionism requires taking small, actionable steps. Breaking tasks into manageable parts creates clarity and reduces overwhelm, helping you steadily progress without fixation on perfection.

5.6 Failure as Feedback: Learning to Pivot, Not Perish

Imagine finishing a project and feeling like it fell short of your expectations. Instead of seeing it as a definitive failure, consider changing the narrative around failure itself. Think of it as valuable feedback, a critical part of your learning curve, rather than a negative endpoint. This mindset shift can transform how you approach setbacks, helping you see them as opportunities for growth and improvement. By reframing failure, you start recognizing that each misstep provides important information on what works and what doesn't, guiding you toward better choices in the future.

Learning from mistakes involves extracting lessons from each experience and turning them into actionable steps toward success. Start by reflecting on what went wrong and why. Ask yourself questions like, "What could I have done differently?" and "What did this experience teach me?" This self-reflection helps you identify patterns and areas for improvement. It's not about dwelling on the mistake but understanding it well enough to make informed changes. For instance, if a presentation didn't go as planned because of poor time management, you can work on allocating your time more effectively next time. This approach turns every mistake into a stepping stone toward your goals.

Pivoting strategies are essential for using feedback from failures to make strategic adjustments. When you encounter setbacks, use the feedback to reassess your approach, goals, or methods. This might involve changing your tactics, setting more realistic targets, or even shifting your focus entirely. For example, if you're working on a business venture that isn't gaining traction, consider pivoting your strategy. Maybe your target market needs reevaluation, or your marketing tactics require a fresh perspective. By staying flexible and open to change, you can use failure as a guide, steering you toward more effective solutions and ultimately achieving better outcomes.

To apply these principles in your daily life, practice adopting a mindset that views setbacks as temporary and surmountable. Each time you face a challenge, remind yourself this is part of the process. Embrace the idea that failure is not the end but a critical component of your journey toward success. Use the lessons learned to refine your approach and keep moving forward with resilience and determination.

As you continue to embrace these mindset shifts, setbacks will become less daunting. They will transform into valuable opportunities for growth, helping you navigate life's challenges with greater confidence and adaptability.

Shifting from a fixed mindset to a growth mindset frees you to see mistakes as lessons and effort as progress rather than proof of inadequacy. This change softens perfectionism by celebrating growth over flawlessness. In the next chapter, we'll apply specific tools—like the CALM method—to make these shifts part of your everyday life.

Chapter 6

Strategies to Curb Perfectionism

I magine yourself at your desk, facing a never-ending to-do list. Each task seems insurmountable because you're not just striving to complete it—you're striving for perfection. This unyielding quest for perfection can be draining and paralyzing. It's time to introduce a more compassionate and balanced approach. Enter the CALM method, a four-step strategy designed to help you manage and diminish perfectionism.

6.1 The CALM Method: A Four-Step Approach to Reducing Perfectionism

The first step is to **Capture Your Thoughts**. Imagine you're working on a project, and suddenly, a critical thought pops into your head: "This isn't good enough." Instead of letting this thought fester, write it down. Use a journal or a digital note app to capture these perfectionist thoughts as they arise. Externalizing your thoughts helps you see them more objectively. When you write them down, you can evaluate whether these thoughts are realistic or simply your perfectionism talking. This process of capturing and evaluating your thoughts can be incredibly freeing, as it allows you to distance yourself from the immediate emotional impact and see things more clearly.

Then, it's time to **Accept Imperfections**. This step is about changing how you view mistakes. Instead of seeing them as failures, start viewing them as opportunities for growth and learning. Let's say you've made an error in a report. Rather than beating yourself up, ask yourself, "What can I learn from this?" Accepting imperfections in yourself and others can significantly reduce the stress and anxiety associated with perfectionism. Practice reframing your thoughts: instead of "I failed," think "I learned something valuable." This shift in perspective can make a world of difference in how you handle setbacks, turning them from burdens into stepping stones.

Letting Go of Control is the third step. Perfectionists often feel the need to control every outcome, which can be incredibly stressful and exhausting. One way to alleviate this is by delegating tasks. Trusting others and their abilities can be challenging, but it's essential for reducing your workload and stress levels. Start small—delegate minor tasks and gradually move on to more significant responsibilities. Let go of the need to micromanage and focus on the bigger picture. This shift can help you realize that outcomes don't always have to be perfect to be successful. Allowing others to contribute can also bring fresh perspectives and innovative solutions that you might not have considered.

Finally, integrate **Mindfulness Practice** into your daily routine. Mindfulness helps you stay present and aware, reducing the constant worry about achieving perfection. Simple practices like meditation and deep breathing can make a significant difference. Dedicate a few minutes each day to sit quietly and focus on your breath. When perfectionist thoughts arise, acknowledge them without judgment and gently bring your attention back to the present moment. Over time, these mindfulness practices can help you develop a more balanced and compassionate mindset, allowing you to let go of the need for perfection and embrace a more fulfilling way of living.

6.2 Mindfulness Techniques for Everyday Situations

Picture this: you're about to walk into an important meeting, and your heart is pounding. You feel the familiar tension building up. This is where mindful breathing can be a game-changer. A quick technique called "box breathing" can help calm your nerves. Inhale deeply for four counts, hold the breath for four counts, exhale for four counts, and then hold the empty breath for another four counts. Repeat this cycle a few times, and you'll notice a significant reduction in stress. This method not only helps you stay calm but also brings your focus back to the present moment, making it easier to handle whatever comes next.

Now, imagine taking a short break from your desk and going for a walk. But instead of letting your mind race with worries, you engage in mindful walking. Focus on each step, the sensation of your feet touching the ground, the rhythm of your breath, and the sounds around you. Even a five-minute walk like this can foster a greater appreciation for the present moment and lessen the grip of perfectionist thinking. It's a simple yet powerful way to reset your mind, helping you return to your tasks with a fresh perspective and reduced anxiety.

Eating mindfully is another technique that can bring a sense of calm and presence to your day. In our busy lives, meals often become just another task to rush through. Instead, try to pay full attention to the experience of eating. Notice the colors, textures, and flavors of your food. Chew slowly and savor each bite. This practice not only enhances your enjoyment of food but also helps you slow down and appreciate small moments. It's a reminder that not everything needs to be done quickly or perfectly; sometimes, simply being present is enough.

Mindful listening can transform your interactions with others. Whether in a meeting or a casual conversation, make it a point to fully engage with the person speaking. Put away distractions, maintain eye contact, and focus entirely on their words and emotions. This practice ensures you stay present and fully engaged, enhancing the quality of your connections. It also reduces the tendency to overthink your responses or worry about how you're being perceived. By truly listening, you create a space for genuine understanding and empathy, which can strengthen your relationships and alleviate the pressure to be perfect.

6.3 Navigating the Digital World with Mindfulness

Imagine scrolling through your social media feed. You see perfectly curated photos of vacations, flawless home decor, and seemingly effortless successes. It's hard not to compare your life to these snapshots and feel like you're falling short. This curated nature of social media can intensify perfectionistic tendencies, making you feel like you have to match those unrealistic standards. The constant exposure to idealized images can negatively impact your self-esteem, leading you to believe that your real, unfiltered life is inadequate. Social comparison on these platforms can create a vicious cycle of striving for unattainable perfection, leaving you feeling stressed and unworthy.

Using social media mindfully and intentionally can help mitigate these adverse effects. Start by curating your feed to include positive and realistic content. Follow accounts that promote authenticity and self-acceptance rather than perfection. Limit your time on social platforms by setting specific time slots for social media use. This can prevent you from falling down the rabbit hole of endless scrolling. Practice critical thinking about what you see online. Remember that most people share their highlights, not their struggles. This awareness can help you maintain a healthier perspective and reduce the impact of perfectionism.

Setting personal boundaries around social media use is crucial for protecting your mental health. Designate specific times to check your social media accounts and stick to them. For example, you might decide to check your feeds only in the morning and evening, avoiding midday distractions. Unfollow accounts that trigger perfectionistic thoughts. If certain profiles make you feel inadequate or stressed, it's okay to remove them from your feed. Regularly take breaks from digital platforms. A digital detox, even for a day, can provide a refreshing break and help you reconnect with the real world. These steps can help you maintain a balanced perspective and prevent social media from exacerbating perfectionist tendencies.

Engaging with supportive digital communities can also be beneficial. Seek out or create online spaces that promote self-acceptance, authentic connections, and positive change. Join groups or follow hashtags focusing on mental health, self-compassion, and real-life experiences. These communities can provide a sense of belonging and help dismantle perfectionistic thinking. Actively participate in discussions and share your own experiences. This engagement can foster a sense of connection and support, reducing the isolation often accompanying perfectionism. By engaging in these supportive spaces, balancing social media use can help you maintain a healthier relationship with digital platforms and foster a sense of community, making you feel connected and understood in your digital journey.

Navigating the digital world mindfully involves being intentional about how you use social media and setting boundaries to protect your mental health. This balanced approach can help you appreciate social media's positive aspects while minimizing its potential to fuel unrealistic expectations and self-critical thoughts.

6.4 Using Technology and Apps to Manage Perfectionist Tendencies

Navigating the demands of daily life can be overwhelming, especially when perfectionism looms over every task. Thankfully, technology offers tools to help manage your time and reduce stress. Productivity apps like Trello and Asana are game-changers for organizing tasks. These apps allow you to break down projects into smaller, manageable steps, setting realistic deadlines along the way. Imagine you have a major report due; by using Trello, you can create a board that lists all the sections you need to complete, assigning due dates and priorities to each. This visual organization helps you see your progress and reduces the anxiety of tackling a massive project all at once.

Mindfulness and meditation apps are another powerful ally. Apps like Headspace and Calm provide guided meditations and exercises specifically designed to reduce stress and anxiety. Picture yourself at the end of a long day, feeling the weight of unmet perfectionist standards. Opening the Calm app, you find a guided meditation that helps you focus on your breath and let go of the day's worries. These sessions can be as short as five minutes, making it easy to fit into your busy schedule. Regularly using these apps can help you develop a mindfulness practice, creating moments of calm and clarity amidst the chaos.

Building healthy routines without the pressure of perfection can be challenging. Still, habit-tracking apps like Habitica and Streaks make it easier. These apps gamify the process of forming new habits, turning it into a fun and rewarding experience. For instance, Habitica allows you to create a character and earn rewards for completing daily tasks and habits. If you're trying to build a habit of daily exercise, you can set it up in Habitica and earn points for each day you complete your workout. This approach makes habit formation more engaging and less about achieving perfection, focusing instead on consistent effort and progress.

Emotional wellness apps like Moodpath and Daylio offer a way to monitor and reflect on your mental state. These apps prompt you to log your mood and activities throughout the day, helping you identify patterns and triggers related to perfectionist behaviors. Imagine a particularly tough day where you felt overwhelmed by the need to get everything right. Logging your feelings in Moodpath, you might notice that your stress peaks during specific tasks or times of the day. Over time, this data can provide valuable insights, allowing you to adjust and develop strategies to manage your perfectionist tendencies more effectively.

Using a combination of these apps, you can create a supportive digital environment that helps you manage perfectionism. Productivity apps keep you organized and focused, mindfulness apps offer moments of calm, habit-tracking apps make building new routines enjoyable, and emotional wellness apps provide insights into your mental health. Together, they create a toolkit that supports your well-being and helps you navigate the complexities of daily life with greater ease and balance.

6.5 Setting Achievable Goals: The SMARTER Way

Imagine you're trying to tackle a massive project at work. Without breaking it down, this can feel overwhelming. Defining goals with clear details transforms daunting tasks into manageable milestones, such as 'complete the research by Wednesday' or 'draft the introduction by Friday.'

Once you have specific goals, the next step is to ensure they are **measurable**. Clear metrics for success help you track your progress and stay motivated. For instance, if your goal is to improve your fitness, set measurable targets like "run three times a week for 30 minutes" or "increase my bench press by 10 pounds in two months." These metrics allow you to see tangible progress, which can be incredibly motivating and affirming.

Setting **achievable** goals is a crucial strategy to prevent feelings of failure and frustration. While setting sky-high goals may be tempting, it's essential to be realistic about what you can accomplish within a given timeframe. For instance, if learning a new language is your goal, start with a manageable target like "learn 50 new words this month" rather than aiming to "become fluent in three months." Achievable goals keep you motivated and help you build momentum, making it more likely that you'll stick with your plans.

Your goals should also be **relevant**, meaning they align with your personal values and long-term objectives. Pursuing goals for external validation can lead to burnout and dissatisfaction. Reflect on what truly matters to you. If career growth is important, ensure your goals align with this value. Instead of setting a goal to "get a promotion to impress others," choose "develop leadership skills to advance my career." This relevance ensures your goals are personally meaningful, making them more fulfilling and easier to commit to.

Time-bound goals provide structure and a sense of urgency without overwhelming pressure. Assigning a realistic timeframe to each goal helps you stay on track and manage your time effectively. For example, if your goal is to write a book, break it down into time-bound steps like "write one chapter per month." This approach helps you avoid procrastination and keeps your momentum going, as you have clear deadlines to work towards.

Regularly **evaluating** your progress is essential to keep your goals on track. Set aside time to review your achievements and identify areas where you might need to adjust your approach. This evaluation helps you stay focused and ensures your goals remain relevant and achievable. If you notice that a particular strategy isn't working, don't be afraid to make changes. Flexibility is key to maintaining motivation and engagement.

Finally, be willing to **re-adjust** your goals based on feedback and changing circumstances. Life is unpredictable, and sticking rigidly to a plan can lead to unnecessary stress. If you encounter obstacles, take them as opportunities to reassess and refine your goals. This flexible approach allows you to adapt to new challenges and keep moving forward, maintaining a balance between ambition and well-being.

6.6 Overcoming Perfectionist Habits Through Flexibility

Embracing flexibility in your daily routines can make a significant difference in managing perfectionist tendencies. The rigidity of a strict routine can add unnecessary stress, as it often leaves little room for error or spontaneity. Allowing for flexibility means understanding that not every day will go as planned, and that's perfectly okay. For instance, if you have a morning routine involving a specific order of tasks—like exercise, meditation, and breakfast—give yourself permission to switch it up if needed. Maybe today, you start with breakfast because you woke up hungrier than usual, and that's fine. This flexibility reduces the pressure to perform perfectly every single day and helps you adapt more easily to life's inevitable disruptions.

Regularly assessing and adapting your routines based on current needs and life changes is crucial. Life is dynamic, and what worked for you last month might not be as effective today. For example, suppose you've recently taken on new responsibilities at work. In that case, your old routine might need tweaking to accommodate these changes. Take time every few weeks to evaluate your daily schedule. Ask yourself if it still aligns with your goals and well-being. If not, make adjustments. This could mean shifting your workout time to the evening or incorporating short breaks throughout your day. By staying attuned to your evolving circumstances, you foster a more relaxed approach to your daily tasks, reducing the rigidity that perfectionism thrives on.

Focusing on progress rather than perfection within your routines can be incredibly liberating. The purpose of having a routine is to support your well-being, not to create additional pressure. Celebrate small victories and incremental improvements. If your goal is to read more, don't stress if you miss a day. Focus on the fact that you've read more this week than you did last month. This shift in perspective allows you to appreciate your progress without getting bogged down by the occasional slip-up. Remember, consistency is more important than perfection. The more you practice valuing progress, the less power perfectionism will hold over you.

We introduced practical methods to dismantle perfectionistic thinking, from mindfulness hacks to setting healthy boundaries. By experimenting with these strategies, you reclaim mental space and find balance. Next, we'll look at how to let go of "perfect" in daily activities and discover the unexpected joy in imperfection.

Make a Difference with Your Review

Unlock the Power of Generosity

> "Happiness never decreases by being shared."
>
> -Buddha

People who give without expecting anything back are happier. Let's make a difference together!

Can you help someone like you who wants to feel happier but doesn't know where to start?

My goal is to make the journey from perfectionism to happiness lighter and easier for everyone.

But to reach more people, I need your help.

Most people choose books based on reviews. So, I'm asking you to help another perfectionist by leaving a review.

It's free, takes less than a minute, and could truly change someone's life.

Your review might help :

...one more person feel less anxious.

...one more family build stronger relationships.

...one more student enjoy school without fear of mistakes.

...one more parent feel good about themselves.

To make a difference, simply scan the QR code below and leave a review :

(for paperback)

or, for ebook >>> Click here to leave your review on Amazon

Chapter 7

Embracing Imperfection in Daily Life

You're watching a child gleefully build a sandcastle at the beach. Each wave that washes over their creation is met with laughter and determination to rebuild it. There's no frustration, just pure enjoyment in the process. This child-like embrace of unpredictability is something we can all learn from, especially when it comes to our hobbies and recreational activities. Engaging in activities that thrive on unpredictability can be incredibly liberating for a perfectionist.

7.1 Thriving on Unpredictability in Hobbies and Recreation

Consider gardening, for instance. It's a hobby that inherently involves elements of unpredictability, from weather conditions to soil quality. You plant seeds hoping they'll grow, but you can't control every factor. Gardening teaches patience and adaptability as you learn to work with nature rather than against it. Similarly, fishing is another activity steeped in unpredictability. You can spend hours waiting for a bite, enjoying the tranquility of nature and the thrill of the unexpected. The experience is less about the catch and more about being present and appreciating the moment.

Playing improvisational music is another fantastic example. Unlike reading sheet music, improv requires you to adapt and respond in real time, making it a powerful exercise in letting go. Each note played is a decision made in the moment, with no time for overthinking or self-criticism. This spontaneous creativity can be incredibly freeing, allowing you to express yourself without the burden of perfection.

Pursuing new interests without the pressure to excel can be a game-changer. When trying something new, focus on the joy of learning rather than the outcome. For instance, if you've always wanted to try painting, don't worry about creating a masterpiece. Instead, enjoy the process of mixing colors and putting brush to canvas. The same goes for activities like dancing, where the goal is to move and have fun rather than perfect each step. By stepping out of your comfort zone and embracing new experiences, you open yourself up to growth and self-discovery.

Moments of frustration are inevitable in any hobby, but they don't have to derail your enjoyment. When you find yourself getting frustrated, take a break. Step away for a few minutes, take deep breaths, and return with a fresh perspective. That's also where the CALM approach from Chapter 6.1 can help: Capture any self-critical thoughts, Accept that mistakes happen, Let go of rigid outcomes, and remain Mindful of the learning process. Setting realistic expectations is also crucial. Understand that progress takes time and mistakes are part of the learning process. Instead of aiming for perfection, value incremental improvements. For example, if you're learning to play an instrument, celebrate mastering a new chord rather than expecting to play a complex piece flawlessly.

Frustration Management Tips

Managing Frustration in Hobbies:

1. Take Breaks: When frustration peaks, step away and clear your mind.

2. Set Realistic Goals: Break down your hobby into manageable tasks.

3. Celebrate Small Wins: Acknowledge and celebrate even the smallest progress.

4. Stay Present: Focus on the process rather than the outcome.

By incorporating these tips, you can transform moments of frustration into opportunities for growth and enjoyment.

Embracing unpredictability in hobbies can lead to a more fulfilling and balanced life. These activities teach resilience, patience, and the ability to adapt—valuable skills that extend beyond the hobby itself. So, whether you're tending to a garden, casting a fishing line, or jamming on a guitar, allow yourself to enjoy the journey, imperfections and all.

7.2 Imperfection and Creativity: Liberating the Creative Mind

Imagine you're staring at a blank canvas, brush in hand, feeling the pressure to create something flawless. The fear of making a mistake can be paralyzing, stifling your creativity before you even begin. Embracing imperfection can be a game-changer. When you let go of the need to be perfect, you free yourself to take risks and explore new ideas without the fear of failure. This openness can lead to greater creativity as you allow yourself to experiment and innovate. Perfectionism often limits you to safe, predictable choices, but embracing flaws can open up a world of creative possibilities.

Consider the story of Jackson Pollock, a renowned abstract expressionist painter. Pollock's technique of dripping and splattering paint was revolutionary, and it came from his willingness to embrace imperfection. His unconventional methods allowed him to create dynamic, expressive works that broke away from traditional painting techniques. Pollock once said, "I don't use the accident; I deny the accident." This mindset of seeing value in unexpected outcomes can lead to breakthroughs in your creative process. Similarly, writers like Ernest Hemingway embraced imperfection. Hemingway famously rewrote the ending of "A Farewell to Arms" 39 times before he was satisfied. He understood that the revision process, with all its flaws and changes, was crucial to producing his best work.

Another inspiring example is the musician Miles Davis, who revolutionized jazz by embracing imperfection and spontaneity. Davis often encouraged his band members to make mistakes, believing these "wrong" notes could lead to new, innovative sounds. This approach allowed for a fluid, ever-evolving style that became a hallmark of his music. Davis's philosophy highlights the importance of seeing mistakes not as failures but as opportunities for creative growth. These case studies show that many successful creatives attribute their achievements to embracing flaws and unexpected outcomes in their work.

If you're looking to boost your creative thinking, try engaging in exercises that encourage expression without judgment. Free writing is an excellent starting point. Set a timer for ten minutes and write whatever comes to mind without censoring yourself. Don't worry about grammar or coherence; just let the words flow. This exercise can help you break through mental blocks and tap into your subconscious thoughts. Improvisational drawing is another great activity. Grab a sketchpad and some pencils, and let your hand move freely across the paper. Don't aim for a finished product; instead, enjoy creating without a plan. The goal is to explore and experiment without the pressure of producing something perfect.

Spontaneous photography can also be incredibly liberating. Take your camera or smartphone and go for a walk, capturing whatever catches your eye. Don't spend time setting up the perfect shot; instead, focus on capturing moments and details that intrigue you. This practice can help you see beauty in the unexpected and develop a more relaxed approach to your creative work. By engaging in these exercises, you can cultivate a mindset that values the creative process over the final product, freeing yourself from the constraints of perfectionism and allowing your creativity to flourish.

7.3 Creating Content Without Perfectionism: A Guide for Digital Creators

Imagine you're staring at your computer screen, ready to hit publish on a blog post you've been refining for days. Your heart races as you wonder whether it meets the mark—did you miss something? Will the audience catch every little flaw? This is a typical struggle for digital creators. The need for everything to be perfect can be paralyzing, keeping you from sharing your work with the world. Overcoming these perfectionist challenges starts with recognizing that your content doesn't need to be flawless to be valuable. Strive for authenticity and connection rather than unattainable perfection. Your audience is more likely to connect with genuine, relatable content than with something overly polished but lacking personality.

Authenticity over perfection is crucial in content creation. In a world inundated with highly edited images and scripted videos, what resonates most with audiences is realness. People crave content that feels genuine and showcase the human side of the creator. Think about your favorite YouTubers or bloggers. Chances are, they're not perfect, but their authenticity makes them relatable and trustworthy. Sharing your true self, including your imperfections, can build a stronger connection with your audience. They appreciate knowing that you're human, just like them, and that your content comes from a place of sincerity.

Dealing with criticism is an inevitable part of putting yourself out there. The internet can be a harsh place, and it's easy for negative comments to fuel your perfectionist tendencies. However, it's important to handle criticism constructively. Start by separating the constructive feedback from the trolling. Constructive criticism can be a valuable tool for growth, offering insights you might not have considered. When you receive such feedback, take a moment to process it without reacting defensively. Reflect on whether there's merit to the critique and how you can use it to improve your content. On the other hand, negative comments that are purely hurtful should be taken with a grain of salt. Remember, not everyone's opinion reflects your value or the quality of your work.

Balancing creativity and productivity is another challenge for digital creators. It's easy to get caught up in the creative process, endlessly tweaking your work in pursuit of perfection. However, this can lead to burnout and decreased productivity. Finding a healthy middle ground involves setting clear boundaries for your creative sessions. Allocate specific times for brainstorming and creating and separate times for editing and refining. This structure can help you stay focused and ensure that you're making consistent progress without getting bogged down by perfectionism. Embracing deadlines, even self-imposed ones, can also be beneficial. They push you to complete your work within a reasonable timeframe, preventing the endless cycle of revisions.

Remember, your audience values content that speaks to them, even if it's not perfect. So, hit that publish button, share your work, and know that your authenticity is what truly matters.

7.4 The Beauty of Imperfect Housekeeping

Picture the pressure to maintain a pristine home, where every corner must be spotless, every item in its place. Society often dictates that a perfect home reflects a well-organized, successful life. But this relentless pursuit of a flawless living space can become a source of stress and anxiety. It's time to challenge these societal norms and propose a more relaxed approach that prioritizes comfort and practicality over perfection. Imagine a home where the focus is on creating a welcoming, lived-in atmosphere rather than a showroom. This shift can transform your living space into a sanctuary reflecting your personality and lifestyle rather than a space constantly demanding upkeep.

Consider the beauty of a 'lived-in' home. These spaces tell stories, showcasing personal artifacts, cherished memories, and even the occasional mess. A stack of books on the coffee table, family photos on the fridge, and a cozy blanket draped over the couch—all these elements add warmth and character. Instead of striving for sterile perfection, embrace the little imperfections that make your home uniquely yours. These lived-in touches create a more welcoming and stress-free environment for you and your guests. When visitors see a house that feels real and lived-in, they feel more at ease and connected. It's the difference between walking into a museum and stepping into a friend's cozy living room.

Practical organization tips can help balance tidiness with ease of use. Open shelving is a fantastic option for frequently used items, making them easily accessible while adding a decorative element to your space. Think of a kitchen shelf lined with colorful mugs or a living room shelf displaying your favorite books and knick-knacks. Baskets are another great solution for quick clean-ups. They can hold anything from kids' toys to magazines, keeping clutter at bay while remaining within reach. Designate a basket in each room for collecting items that need to be put away later. This way, you can maintain a tidy appearance without the stress of constant cleaning. Additionally, consider using storage ottomans or benches to keep items out of sight but still easily accessible, or invest in multi-functional furniture that can serve both practical and decorative purposes.

Reducing the pressure to maintain a perfect home can have significant mental health benefits. When you let go of the need for flawless presentation, you free up mental energy for more fulfilling activities. The constant stress of keeping everything immaculate can lead to increased anxiety and a sense of failure when things aren't perfect. By embracing a more relaxed approach, you create a home environment that supports your well-being. A space where you can unwind without worrying about every little detail being in place. This shift can lead to greater overall happiness, as your home becomes a true haven rather than a source of stress.

Imagine coming home after a long day, kicking off your shoes, and sinking into your sofa without a second thought about the pile of mail on the table or the shoes by the door. This is the essence of a relaxed home environment—a space that welcomes you, imperfections and all. It's about creating a balance where your home is functional, comfortable, and reflective of your life's beautiful chaos. So, let go of the societal pressure for perfection and embrace the beauty of a lived-in, imperfect home.

7.5 Dressing for Comfort and Confidence, Not Perfection

You're standing in front of your closet, agonizing over what to wear. Society has ingrained the idea that perfect attire equates to respect and professionalism. But let's challenge this notion. Dressing perfectly isn't a prerequisite for being taken seriously or feeling confident. Prioritizing comfort and self-expression in your wardrobe choices can be liberating. When you wear clothes that feel good and align with your personal style, you naturally exude confidence. Think about it: ever notice how much more productive and positive you feel when you're comfortable in what you're wearing? The pressure to conform to an ideal of "perfect" dressing can be stifling, but letting go of that can make your daily routine much more enjoyable.

Developing a personal style that reflects your identity and values is a rewarding journey. Start by exploring what makes you feel most like yourself. Do you gravitate towards bold colors, or are you more comfortable in neutral tones? Do you prefer structured outfits or more relaxed, casual wear? Don't be afraid to experiment. Try on different styles and observe how they make you feel. It's not about following the latest fashion trends but discovering what resonates with you personally. Your wardrobe should be a reflection of who you are, not what others expect you to be. Consider creating a mood board with images and fabrics that inspire you. This can guide you in curating a wardrobe that feels authentically yours.

Clothing choices have a profound impact on mental well-being. Dressing in a way that prioritizes comfort and personal taste can significantly improve your mood and self-esteem. Imagine the difference between wearing a stiff, uncomfortable outfit versus something soft and cozy that makes you feel good. The latter choice can uplift your spirits and give you a sense of ease and assurance throughout your day. This shift in how you approach dressing can reduce the pressure to meet societal standards, allowing you to focus more on how you feel rather than how you're perceived. It's a subtle but powerful form of self-care that can make a huge difference in your daily life.

To make this practical, start by paying attention to how you feel in different outfits. Keep a journal for a week, noting which clothes make you feel confident and comfortable versus those that leave you feeling self-conscious or uncomfortable. This exercise can help you identify patterns and preferences, guiding you in making more mindful wardrobe choices. Additionally, consider decluttering your closet to keep only the items that you truly love and feel great in. This can simplify your daily dressing routine and reduce decision fatigue. Remember, the goal is to dress in a way that makes you feel good, both inside and out.

Incorporating these changes into your wardrobe can transform how you approach dressing, making it a more enjoyable and empowering experience. This shift can have a positive ripple effect on various aspects of your life, boosting your confidence and overall well-being.

7.6 Cooking without the Pressure of Culinary Perfection

Imagine standing in your kitchen, surrounded by fresh ingredients, with no set recipe in mind. Cooking becomes less of a chore and more of an adventure when you embrace the joy of experimentation. Think about the excitement of combining unexpected flavors or the satisfaction of creating a new dish from scratch. Mistakes aren't failures here—they're opportunities. Maybe you accidentally add too much spice, but discover a new favorite flavor profile in the process. Embracing this mindset can turn cooking into a creative and enjoyable activity rather than a stressful task. It's about the journey of cooking, not just the destination.

Focusing on simple, wholesome meals can transform your approach to cooking. Instead of aiming for gourmet presentations, prioritize dishes that nourish both body and soul. Think of a hearty vegetable soup or a simple pasta tossed with fresh tomatoes and herbs. These meals don't require fancy techniques or expensive ingredients but provide comfort and satisfaction. Simple meals can still be delicious and nutritious, offering emotional benefits as well. The act of preparing and eating wholesome food can be grounding and therapeutic, a break from the fast-paced demands of daily life. It's a way to care for yourself and your loved ones without the pressure of culinary perfection.

To make cooking stress-free, preparation is key. Start by organizing your kitchen and prepping ingredients ahead of time. Chop vegetables, marinate proteins, and measure spices before cooking. This saves time and makes the cooking process smoother and more enjoyable. Embrace one-pot meals, which are a lifesaver for busy days. Think of a hearty stew or a flavorful stir-fry combining protein, veggies, and grains in one pot. These dishes are easy to prepare and require minimal cleanup. Slow cookers are another fantastic tool. They allow you to set up your meal in the morning and come home to a delicious, ready-to-eat dinner.

Incorporating these strategies into your cooking routine can help you find joy in the process, reduce stress, and create delicious, wholesome meals without the pressure of perfection. Cooking becomes an act of self-care, a way to nourish yourself and those you love, and a space to experiment and play without fear of failure.

Even in small, routine tasks—like tidying up or picking out clothes—welcoming imperfection can make space for creativity, spontaneity, and relief from constant self-criticism. Next, we'll delve into how perfectionism affects mental and physical well-being—and uncover ways to stay healthy amid life's demands.

Chapter 8

Mental and Physical Health Impacts

Y ou're sitting on your couch, trying to relax after a long day, but your mind won't stop racing. You're replaying every conversation, every task, every little thing that didn't go perfectly. This constant mental chatter isn't just annoying—it's a hallmark of how closely perfectionism and anxiety are linked. The relentless pursuit of flawlessness can drive your anxiety through the roof, making it nearly impossible to unwind or feel at ease. Perfectionism isn't just about high standards; it's about a deep-seated fear of making mistakes, which can trigger significant anxiety responses.

8.1 The Anxiety-Perfectionism Link: Understanding and Management

Perfectionism often leads to heightened anxiety because the fear of not meeting expectations or making mistakes is a constant companion. Imagine waking up each day with a checklist of tasks that must be done perfectly. The pressure to meet these self-imposed standards can be overwhelming. This fear isn't just abstract; it manifests physically and emotionally, leading to symptoms that disrupt your daily life. Constant worry is common among perfectionists, creating a state of perpetual anxiety. You might find yourself obsessing over details others wouldn't even notice, from the wording in an email to the alignment of a picture frame. This incessant worry can make even the simplest tasks feel insurmountable, leaving you mentally exhausted. If you catch yourself spiraling, recall the CALM method from Chapter 6.1: Capture anxious thoughts, Accept that mistakes are normal, Let go of impossible standards, and practice Mindfulness to calm your body's stress response.

Insomnia is another frequent symptom. You lie in bed, unable to turn off your thoughts, replaying the day's events or planning how to avoid mistakes tomorrow. This lack of sleep only exacerbates anxiety, creating a vicious cycle. Physical symptoms like headaches and stomachaches are also common. The stress of striving for perfection can cause tension headaches, while the anxiety can lead to digestive issues, making your stomach churn and twist. Even more subtle symptoms, like muscle tension and fatigue, can creep in, leaving you feeling physically drained and mentally frazzled. This constant state of tension and worry can significantly affect your overall well-being.

Managing anxiety related to perfectionism involves several strategies, starting with cognitive restructuring. This technique helps you challenge and reframe perfectionist thoughts. For example, instead of thinking, "I must get this project perfect, or I'll fail," try, "I'll do my best, and that's enough." This shift in perspective can reduce the pressure you place on yourself and alleviate anxiety. It's about recognizing that mistakes don't define your worth and that imperfection is a natural part of being human. This cognitive shift can be reinforced through journaling, where you write down your perfectionist thoughts and actively challenge them with more balanced, realistic perspectives. This process gives you a sense of control over your thoughts and feelings, empowering you to manage your anxiety.

Relaxation practices are also crucial. Deep breathing exercises can be incredibly effective in calming your mind and reducing anxiety. Try the 4-7-8 technique: inhale for four seconds, hold your breath for seven, and exhale for eight. This practice can help slow your heart rate and reduce the physical symptoms of anxiety. Progressive muscle relaxation is another helpful technique. By tensing and slowly releasing each muscle group, you can release physical tension and promote relaxation. This practice helps with anxiety and improves your overall sense of well-being.

An interactive element that can be particularly helpful is creating a relaxation routine. Set aside time each day for activities that help you unwind, such as reading a book, listening to calming music, practicing yoga or tai chi, or doing mindfulness meditation. This routine can serve as a buffer against the daily stressors that fuel perfectionist anxiety. Additionally, consider incorporating visualization techniques, where you imagine a peaceful scene or a successful outcome, to combat negative thoughts. Over time, these practices can help you build resilience against anxiety and reduce the grip of perfectionism on your life.

8.2 Perfectionism and Its Role in Chronic Stress and Fatigue

You're pushing yourself to complete a project at work, staying up late and skipping meals to get everything right. This constant drive for perfection isn't just mentally draining—it's a prime example of chronic stress. Chronic stress is more than just feeling frazzled for a day or two. It's a prolonged state of stress that lingers and can lead to serious health issues. Imagine your body is always in "fight-or-flight" mode, with your heart rate and blood pressure constantly elevated. Over time, this constant state of alertness can wear down your cardiovascular system, increasing the risk of heart disease. Your immune system also takes a hit, making you more susceptible to illnesses. Chronic stress can even affect your digestive system, leading to problems like acid reflux or irritable bowel syndrome.

Perfectionism is a significant contributor to chronic stress. The relentless drive to meet impossibly high standards means you're never fully satisfied with your accomplishments. Every success feels incomplete; every task could have been done better. This never-ending cycle keeps you in constant stress, where relaxation feels impossible. Even after completing a project, your mind quickly shifts to what's next, never allowing you a moment to breathe. This continuous pressure can lead to burnout, where your mental, emotional, and physical resources are completely drained. You might find yourself unable to enjoy activities you once loved, feeling like you're always running on empty.

One of the most debilitating aspects of chronic stress is chronic fatigue syndrome. This isn't just about feeling tired after a long day; it's a persistent exhaustion that doesn't go away with rest. You might wake up feeling just as tired as when you went to bed. Concentration becomes a struggle, making it hard to focus on tasks or remember details. Muscle pain is another common symptom, often accompanied by headaches and joint pain. It feels like your body is constantly aching, and no amount of sleep seems to help. This physical toll can make even simple daily activities feel like monumental tasks, adding to the mental strain of perfectionism.

To combat chronic stress and fatigue, lifestyle changes and stress management techniques are crucial. Start with time management. Break your tasks into manageable chunks and set realistic deadlines. This reduces the overwhelming feeling of having to do everything perfectly all at once. Setting realistic goals is also essential. Instead of aiming for perfection, focus on doing your best within a reasonable timeframe. This shift in mindset can alleviate some of the pressure you place on yourself, making tasks feel more achievable.

Incorporating regular physical activity into your routine can significantly reduce stress and improve your energy levels. Exercise releases endorphins, which are natural mood lifters. Find activities you enjoy, whether a brisk walk, a yoga session, or a dance class. Physical activity doesn't have to be intense to be effective. Even moderate exercise can help reduce stress hormones, improve sleep, and increase overall well-being.

Another effective approach is practicing mindfulness. Mindfulness techniques, such as meditation or deep breathing exercises, can help calm your mind and reduce stress. These practices encourage you to stay present in the moment rather than worrying about past mistakes or future tasks. They help create a mental space where you can relax and recharge.

Lastly, don't underestimate the power of social support. Talking to friends or family about your struggles can provide emotional relief and perspective. Sometimes, just knowing that others understand and support you can make a significant difference. If you find it hard to manage stress on your own, consider seeking professional help. Therapy can give you tools and strategies to cope with stress and perfectionism more effectively.

8.3 Nutritional Self-Care: Eating Well without the Stress

You're standing in your kitchen, staring at a fridge full of ingredients and feeling utterly overwhelmed. The pressure to eat perfectly—to follow the latest diet trends, count every calorie, and avoid every "bad" food—can be paralyzing. Yet, balanced nutrition is crucial for managing stress. What you eat directly impacts your mood, energy levels, and overall health. Consuming a well-rounded diet helps stabilize your mood by maintaining steady blood sugar levels, which can prevent those mid-afternoon energy crashes that leave you feeling irritable and anxious. Foods rich in vitamins and minerals, such as fruits, vegetables, whole grains, and lean proteins, provide the essential nutrients your brain needs to function optimally.

To make healthy eating less stressful, consider some simple, practical tips. Start by planning your meals ahead of time. This doesn't mean you need to create a rigid meal plan, but having a general idea of what you'll eat during the week can save you from last-minute decisions that often lead to unhealthy choices. Focus on whole foods, which are minimally processed and closer to their natural state. These foods are typically more nutritious and satisfying than their heavily processed counterparts. Incorporate mindful eating practices into your routine. This means taking the time to savor your food and paying attention to the flavors, textures, and aromas. Not only does this enhance your enjoyment of meals, but

it also helps prevent overeating by allowing you to recognize when you're truly fu
ll.

Perfectionism often seeps into dietary habits, creating an all-or-nothing mindset.
You might feel that if you can't eat perfectly, there's no point in trying at all. This
mentality can lead to cycles of strict dieting followed by binge eating, which only
exacerbates stress and guilt. But here's the liberating truth: you don't have to be
perfect. Challenge the notion of the 'perfect diet' by embracing a more flexible
approach. Understand that occasional indulgences are not failures but a normal
part of a balanced diet. It's okay to enjoy a piece of cake at a birthday party or
order takeout on a busy night. What matters is your overall dietary pattern, not
the perfection of each meal.

One effective way to shift your mindset is to adopt the 80/20 rule. This approach
reduces the pressure to be perfect and makes healthy eating more sustainable.
Aim to eat nutritious, whole foods 80% of the time, and allow yourself to enjoy
less nutritious foods the other 20%. Use this flexibility to explore new foods and
recipes without the fear of deviating from a strict plan. It's about finding a balance
that works for you and supports your well-being without adding unnecessary
stress.

To make this shift more tangible, consider keeping a food journal, not to track
calories or macros, but to note how different foods make you feel. Pay attention
to your energy levels, mood, and satisfaction after meals. This practice can help
you make more intuitive food choices that nourish your body and mind. If you
struggle with rigid dietary rules, reflect on where these beliefs come from. Are they
influenced by societal pressures, past experiences, or internalized perfectionism?
Understanding the root of these thoughts can help you challenge and reframe them
.

Remember, eating well is about nourishment, not punishment. It's about fueling
your body with the nutrients it needs to thrive and allowing yourself the freedom
to enjoy food without guilt. By adopting a balanced and flexible approach to

nutrition, you can reduce the stress associated with eating and create a more positive relationship with food.

8.4 Exercise as Enjoyment, Not Just Achievement

You're lacing up your running shoes, but instead of feeling excited, you're filled with dread. Another run, another attempt to beat your previous time. It's exhausting, not just physically but mentally. What if exercise could be different? What if it was a source of joy rather than just another task to perfect? Imagine finding forms of physical activity you genuinely enjoy that make you feel alive rather than burdened. Perhaps it's dancing to your favorite songs in the living room or a leisurely hike through a forest trail. When you focus on activities that bring you joy, the need for perfection fades away, and exercise becomes something to look forward to rather than dread.

Regular physical activity offers benefits beyond just physical health. It's a powerful tool for improving mental health. Exercise can help reduce symptoms of depression and anxiety, offering a natural way to boost your mood and enhance your overall sense of well-being. When you engage in physical activity, your body releases endorphins, often called "feel-good" hormones. These endorphins can create a sense of euphoria and reduce the perception of pain, acting as a natural antidepressant. Additionally, exercise can enhance self-esteem and cognitive function. The sense of accomplishment after a good workout can bolster your confidence, while the increased blood flow to the brain can improve focus and mental clarity.

Finding enjoyable physical activities is key to making exercise a sustainable part of your routine. If the thought of hitting the gym fills you with dread, explore other options. Dancing is a fantastic way to get moving while having fun. Whether it's a structured dance class or just freestyle dancing at home, it's a great way to exercise without feeling like you're exercising. Hiking offers the dual benefit of physical activity and immersion in nature, which can be incredibly calming. Team sports can also be a great option, providing a social aspect that makes the activity more engaging. The key is to find what makes you happy and keeps you coming back for more.

A mindful approach to exercise can also transform your experience. Instead of focusing on the end goal—whether a certain weight, time, or distance—try concentrating on the sensations you feel during the activity. Pay attention to how your muscles move, the rhythm of your breath, and the feeling of your feet hitting the ground. This shift in focus from outcomes to the experience itself can make exercise feel less like a chore and more like a form of self-care. Mindfulness during exercise enhances enjoyment and helps you stay present, reducing the mental clutter that perfectionism often brings.

One practical technique to incorporate mindfulness into your exercise routine is to set an intention before you start. This intention could be as simple as "I want to feel the joy of movement" or "I am grateful for what my body can do." As you exercise, remind yourself of this intention whenever you catch your mind wandering to thoughts of performance or perfection. Another technique is to practice gratitude during your workout. As you move, think about how your body supports you, how your heart pumps blood, and how your lungs fill with air. This practice can deepen your appreciation for your body and shift the focus from what it looks like to what it can do.

Incorporating enjoyable and mindful physical activities into your routine can transform exercise from a performance task to a source of joy and well-being. By focusing on what makes you happy and staying present, you can create a positive relationship with exercise that supports your mental and physical health.

8.5 Sleep Hygiene for the Overactive Mind

You're lying in bed, staring at the ceiling, your mind racing about everything you need to do tomorrow—or worse, all the things you didn't do perfectly today. This overactive mind can make falling asleep feel like an impossible task. That's where good sleep hygiene comes in. Sleep hygiene refers to the practices and habits that help you consistently get a good night's sleep. It's about creating an environment conducive to sleep and establishing routines that signal your body that it's time to wind down. Maintaining a consistent sleep schedule is a cornerstone of good sleep hygiene. Going to bed and waking up at the same times every day, even on weekends, helps regulate your body's internal clock, making it easier to fall asleep and wake up refreshed.

Perfectionism can wreak havoc on your sleep. The constant replaying of daily events and the worry about tasks left unfinished can make it hard to relax and fall asleep. You might find yourself lying awake, thinking about an earlier conversation, wondering if you said the right thing, or mentally revising a report you've already submitted. This mental overactivity keeps your brain alert, making it difficult to transition into the restful state needed for sleep. The fear of not meeting expectations or making mistakes can also cause frequent awakenings during the night, leading to fragmented and unrefreshing sleep.

Improving your sleep hygiene can help mitigate these disturbances. Start by limiting your exposure to screens before bedtime. The blue light emitted by phones, tablets, and computers can interfere with the production of melatonin, the hormone that regulates sleep. Try to power down at least an hour before bed and engage in relaxing activities instead. Reading a book, listening to calming music, or taking a warm bath can help signal to your body that it's time to wind down. Relaxation techniques like meditation or gentle yoga can also be beneficial. Practicing mindfulness meditation helps calm the mind, reducing the mental clutter that keeps you awake. Gentle yoga stretches can help release physical tension, making it easier to relax fully.

Keeping a sleep diary can be an effective tool for tracking patterns that affect your sleep. Note what time you go to bed, when you wake up, and any awakenings during the night. Record your pre-sleep activities and any factors that might have influenced your sleep quality, such as stress or caffeine intake. Over time, this diary can help you identify habits disrupting your sleep and make necessary adjustments. You might notice that on nights when you skip your usual wind-down routine, it takes longer to fall asleep. You might also find that certain foods or drinks in the evening are affecting your sleep quality.

Adequate sleep is crucial, not just for physical health but also for mental clarity and emotional resilience. When you're well-rested, you're better equipped to handle the challenges of the day without feeling overwhelmed. Good sleep enhances your ability to think clearly, make decisions, and manage stress. It also plays a vital role in emotional regulation, helping you maintain a balanced mood. For perfectionists, achieving adequate sleep can be a game-changer. It provides the mental and emotional resources needed to effectively challenge perfectionist thoughts and behaviors.

We saw that perfectionism often fuels stress, anxiety, and fatigue—yet we also explored habits that protect your mind and body, from rest to mindful eating. Next, you'll gain more advanced tools for breaking free of perfectionism, including deeper mindfulness techniques and strategic approaches to daily challenges.

Chapter 9

Conquering the Perfectionist Mindset: Tools for a Balanced Life

I magine you're sitting at your desk, the glow of your computer screen high-lighting the furrow in your brow. You've been working on the same paragraph for hours, convinced it needs to be absolutely perfect before you can move on. The pressure is suffocating, and the joy you once found in writing has been replaced by relentless self-criticism. What if, instead of tearing yourself apart, you could offer yourself the same kindness and understanding you'd extend to a friend? This is where self-compassion comes in—a powerful tool that can transform your relationship with yourself and help you combat perfectionism.

9.1 The Role of Self-Compassion in Battling Perfectionism

Self-compassion is often misunderstood, so let's clarify what it truly means. Unlike self-esteem, which is about valuing yourself based on your achievements and how you compare to others, self-compassion involves treating yourself with kindness and understanding, especially when you fail or make mistakes. It's not about indulging yourself or letting yourself off the hook; instead, it's about recognizing that everyone makes mistakes and that these mistakes don't define your worth. Self-compassion has three main components: self-kindness, common humanity, and mindfulness. Self-kindness means being gentle with yourself in-stead of harshly critical. Common humanity is the understanding that suffering and imperfection are not unique to you, but part of the shared human experience. This realization can help you feel less isolated and more connected to others. Mindfulness involves being present with your feelings without overidentifying with them or letting them overwhelm you.

The importance of self-compassion in overcoming perfectionism cannot be over-stated. Perfectionism often leads to undue stress and relentless self-criticism, where every mistake feels like a personal failure. When you practice self-com-passion, you allow yourself to accept your imperfections and failures as part of being human. This acceptance reduces the pressure to be perfect and helps you approach challenges with a more balanced perspective. Here, a quick recall of the CALM approach from Chapter 6.1—Capture your negative self-talk, Accept imperfections, Let go of total control, and stay Mindful—can further soften perfectionism's grip alongside self-compassion. By treating yourself kindly, you can reduce the anxiety and stress that come with perfectionistic tendencies. This doesn't mean you'll stop striving for excellence; it means you'll do so in a healthier, more sustainable way. Self-compassion helps you build resilience, making it easier to bounce back from setbacks and continue pursuing your goals without being crippled by the fear of failure.

Guided self-compassion exercises can be beneficial. Take a moment to find a quiet space where you won't be disturbed. Close your eyes and take a few deep breaths. Think about a recent mistake or failure and notice the emotions that arise. Place your hand over your heart and silently acknowledge your suffering. Say to yourself, "This is a moment of suffering. Suffering is a part of life. May I be kind to myself in this moment. May I give myself the compassion I need." This practice, known as a self-compassion break, can help you stay grounded and kind to yourself during challenging times.

Studies show the positive effects of self-compassion on mental health. Studies have shown that individuals who practice self-compassion experience lower levels of anxiety and depression and higher levels of emotional resilience. According to Dr. Kristin Neff, a leading researcher in self-compassion, this practice can reduce the symptoms of perfectionism by helping individuals develop a more balanced and forgiving view of their capabilities and limitations. By incorporating self-compassion into your daily life, you can create a more supportive inner dialogue, making it easier to navigate the ups and downs of life without the constant burden of perfectionism.

ACTION BOX : Crafting a Kindness Letter

- Aim: Replace harsh self-judgment with a compassionate perspective.

Method:

1. Pinpoint a recent challenge or mistake that's bothering you.

2. Write a letter as if comforting a close friend—acknowledge the struggle, offer empathy, and reaffirm that mistakes are part of being human.

Example: "I know you're feeling really disappointed about missing that deadline at work. It's okay to feel upset but remember that this doesn't define your abilities. You've accomplished so much and will continue to learn and grow from this experience."

Reminder: Re-read this letter whenever self-blame flares up; it's a tangible anchor for gentler thoughts.

9.2 Letting Go of Control: A Step-by-Step Guide

The need for control often stems from deep-seated fears that perfectionists struggle to confront. You might feel that everything will fall apart if you don't oversee every detail. This fear can be rooted in past experiences where things went wrong because you weren't in control. The underlying anxiety is that making mistakes will lead to failure, judgment, or loss of respect. This constant need to control can create a stressful, rigid environment where you're always on high alert, anticipating potential errors. It's exhausting and ultimately unsustainable.

Identifying areas in your life where you're exerting unnecessary control is the first step toward loosening your grip. Start by taking inventory of your daily activities. Are you the one who has to plan every family outing, ensuring every detail is perfect? Do you micromanage at work, double-checking everyone's tasks? Maybe you even rearrange the kitchen cabinets because no one else does it "right." These behaviors might seem trivial, but they drain your energy and amplify your stress. List these control areas and note how they make you feel. This exercise can be eye-opening, helping you realize how much of your time and mental energy is spent on maintaining this control.

Once you've identified these areas, it's time to take practical steps to release your grip. Start small. Choose one or two tasks you can delegate or entirely let go of. It might be difficult initially, but remember that perfection isn't the goal—balance is. For example, if you're always the one organizing family events, let someone else take the reins for a change. Trust that it will be okay even if it's not done exactly how you would do it. At work, delegate tasks to colleagues and resist the urge to micromanage. Provide clear instructions and trust in their abilities. This doesn't just help you; it also empowers those around you, fostering a more collaborative environment.

Embracing uncertainty is a significant part of this process. Life is inherently unpredictable, and trying to control every aspect only leads to frustration and anxiety. By accepting that not everything will go according to plan, you open yourself up to new possibilities and experiences. This can be incredibly freeing. Imagine you're on a road trip without a strict itinerary. The detours and unexpected stops can lead to some of the most memorable and enjoyable moments. Embracing uncertainty doesn't mean you stop caring; it means you're flexible and open to whatever comes your way.

The benefits of embracing uncertainty extend beyond reducing stress. It can lead to a more fulfilling life by allowing you to focus on what truly matters. When you're not bogged down by the minutiae of control, you can direct your energy toward meaningful activities and relationships. You might find yourself more present in conversations, more engaged in your hobbies, and more connected to your loved ones. Letting go of control can also enhance your problem-solving skills. When you're not fixated on one "right" way to do things, you become more creative and adaptable, finding innovative solutions to challenges.

In summary, understanding the fears that drive your need for control, identifying areas where you can let go, taking practical steps to release your grip, and embracing uncertainty can transform your life. It's about finding a balance that allows you to maintain high standards without the suffocating pressure of perfectionism.

9.3 Overcoming All-or-Nothing Thinking

All-or-nothing thinking, sometimes called black-and-white thinking, is a cognitive distortion where you see situations in extremes. There's no middle ground; everything is either a complete success or a total failure. Imagine you've planned a dinner party, hoping for everything to be perfect. The evening goes well, but the dessert doesn't turn out as expected. Instead of focusing on the great conversations and the delicious main course, you fixate on the "failed" dessert, feeling like the entire evening was a disaster. This type of thinking can be exhausting and disheartening because it leaves no room for partial successes or the positives that exist within imperfections.

This cognitive distortion significantly impacts behavior and decision-making processes. You're more likely to procrastinate when you see the world in black-and-white. The fear of not achieving perfect results can paralyze you, making it hard to start tasks or projects. You might avoid trying new things altogether because the risk of not doing them perfectly seems too high. For example, if you're thinking about learning a new language but fear you won't speak it fluently from the get-go, you might avoid starting altogether. This all-or-nothing mindset also affects your ability to make balanced decisions. You might either overcommit, taking on too much because you believe anything less than giving 100% is unacceptable, or undercommit, avoiding responsibilities because they seem too daunting to complete perfectly.

To counteract all-or-nothing thinking, start by setting incremental goals. Break down larger tasks into smaller, manageable steps. Instead of aiming to write an entire report in one sitting, set a goal to complete the introduction today. Celebrate this small win, acknowledging that progress is valuable even if the task isn't finished. Incremental goals help you see that every step forward is a success, reducing the pressure to achieve perfection immediately. Embracing partial successes can also make a big difference. For instance, if you're working on a fitness goal, celebrate that you made it to the gym three times this week instead of criticizing yourself for not going every day. Recognizing these smaller achievements can build momentum and keep you motivated.

Adopting a continuum mindset involves recognizing that life isn't binary. There's a whole range of outcomes between absolute success and failure. Picture a spectrum where each step forward, no matter how small, is a move in the right direction. This mindset encourages you to see value in the process, not just the end result. For instance, if you're learning to play the guitar, every practice session, even when you struggle with chords, contributes to your overall progress. It's not about playing a perfect song right away; it's about enjoying the learning process and noticing improvements over time.

Imagine you're preparing a presentation for work. Instead of aiming for it to be flawless, focus on making it informative and engaging. If you stumble over a few words, remind yourself that the core message is what matters. Embrace the idea that good enough truly is good enough. This shift in perspective can alleviate a lot of the stress and anxiety associated with all-or-nothing thinking. It allows you to be more compassionate with yourself, acknowledging that imperfections are part of the human experience and that they don't diminish your worth or accomplishments.

Finally, practice re-labeling your thoughts. When you catch yourself thinking in extremes, pause and identify the thought as all-or-nothing. Then, reframe it with a more balanced perspective. Instead of thinking, "I always mess up presentations," try, "I had a few slip-ups, but overall, my message was clear and well-received." This simple exercise can help you break the cycle of black-and-white thinking, fostering a more forgiving and realistic mindset.

9.4 The Art of Delegation: Trusting Others to Share the Load

Delegation is often misunderstood. It's not about dumping tasks on someone else or relinquishing control completely. Instead, think of it as a valuable skill that can help you manage your workload and reduce stress. When done right, delegation can make you more effective and allow others to grow. Imagine the relief of sharing the load: you're juggling multiple projects at work, each demanding your undivided attention. Instead of trying to do everything yourself, delegating some tasks can free up your time for what truly requires your expertise.

This principle doesn't just apply to work—it's equally important in your personal life. Delegating tasks to family members, including your husband or wife, can help create a more balanced and cooperative household. It's not about shirking your responsibilities but about sharing them to foster teamwork and mutual support. Whether it's dividing household chores, coordinating childcare, or planning family activities, involving others empowers them while giving you space to focus on your priorities.

Don't overlook children's potential in this equation. Teaching kids to take on age-appropriate responsibilities not only helps lighten your load but also builds their sense of accountability and independence. Simple tasks like tidying their rooms, setting the table, or helping with small chores instill life skills and encourage a spirit of collaboration within the family. When approached collaboratively, delegation strengthens relationships, fosters growth, and reduces stress for everyone involved.

For many perfectionists, the idea of delegation can be daunting. You might fear losing control over the quality of work or worry that others won't meet your high standards. These concerns are valid but manageable. The first step is acknowledging that these fears stem from a need for control and a lack of trust. You might think, "No one can do this as well as I can," but this mindset only adds to your stress and workload. Overcoming these barriers requires a shift in perspective. Start by recognizing that your team or colleagues are capable and that learning to trust them is a process. It's okay if things don't go perfectly the first time; improvement comes with practice and guidance.

Practical strategies for effective delegation can make this process smoother. Begin with clear communication. When you delegate a task, provide detailed instructions and explain the desired outcome. This ensures that the person taking on the task understands your expectations. For example, if you're delegating a report, specify the key points to include, the format you prefer, and the deadline. Setting clear expectations helps avoid misunderstandings and ensures the task is completed to your standards.

Another key strategy is to match tasks with the right people. Consider each team member's strengths and areas for growth. Delegating tasks that align with their skills ensures better results and boosts their confidence and professional development. For instance, if someone excels in data analysis, delegate tasks that play to this strength. This could be analyzing market trends, customer data, or financial reports. If someone is a great communicator, delegate tasks that involve client interactions or team meetings. This not only lightens your load but also empowers them to contribute meaningfully.

Regular check-ins are also crucial. These are not about micromanaging but rather about providing support and guidance. Schedule brief meetings to review progress, address challenges, and offer feedback. This ongoing communication helps keep everyone on the same page and allows you to adjust as needed. It's an opportunity to mentor and support your team, ensuring the task progresses well without constantly looking over their shoulder.

Encouraging a culture of feedback is equally important. After a task is completed, take time to discuss what went well and what could be improved. This constructive feedback loop helps everyone learn and grow. Acknowledge your team's efforts and successes and provide constructive suggestions for improvement. This enhances the quality of work and builds a trusting and collaborative environment.

Lastly, be patient with yourself and others. Delegation is a skill that improves with practice. It may feel uncomfortable initially, but you'll find it more natural with time. Allow room for mistakes and view them as learning opportunities. Remember, the goal is to lighten your load and build a more efficient and cohesive team. By mastering the skill of delegation, you can achieve a better balance, reduce stress, and foster a more productive and positive work environment.

9.5 Embracing Vulnerability: Lessons from Brené Brown

Brené Brown's groundbreaking research on vulnerability and shame provides a fresh perspective on how to counteract perfectionism. According to Brown, vulnerability is the willingness to show up and be seen, even when the outcome is uncertain. It involves putting yourself out there, imperfections and all, and resisting the urge to shield yourself behind a facade of perfection. Brown's work emphasizes that vulnerability is not a weakness but a strength. It's the birthplace of love, belonging, joy, courage, empathy, and creativity. By embracing vulnerability, you can counteract the feelings of shame that often accompany perfectionism. Shame whispers that you'll never measure up, that your flaws define your worth. But vulnerability allows you to connect authentically with others, fostering a sense of belonging and acceptance that can diminish the grip of perfectionism.

The common perception is that vulnerability equates to weakness. Many people, especially perfectionists, believe that showing vulnerabilities will lead to judgment and rejection. This belief can paralyze you from forming genuine connections or taking risks. However, Brown argues that vulnerability is, in fact, a strength. Being open about your fears, mistakes, and imperfections takes immense courage. When you allow yourself to be vulnerable, you give others permission to do the same, creating an environment of mutual support and empathy. This authenticity can lead to deeper, more meaningful relationships. Imagine a leader who admits to their team that they made a mistake. This act of vulnerability can build trust and respect, encouraging a culture where team members feel safe to speak up and take risks without fear of harsh judgment.

To enhance your ability to embrace vulnerability, consider engaging in exercises encouraging openness and authenticity. One effective exercise is to share personal stories or fears in a safe environment. This could be with a trusted friend, family member, or even a support group. Start with something small, like a recent challenge or a mistake you made. Notice how it feels to share and how the other person responds. This practice can help lessen the grip of perfectionism by showing that your worth is not tied to being perfect. Another exercise is to write about a time when you felt vulnerable but showed up anyway. Reflect on what you learned from the experience and how it strengthened your relationships or personal growth.

Another powerful exercise is the "Vulnerability Share" activity. Begin by gathering a small group of trusted individuals. Each person takes a turn sharing a personal story or fear, something that makes them feel vulnerable. The key is to listen without judgment, offering support and understanding. This exercise can be transformative, helping you realize that everyone has vulnerabilities and that sharing them can strengthen bonds and build trust.

Finally, consider practicing guided meditations focused on vulnerability. These meditations can help you become more comfortable with the discomfort that often accompanies vulnerability. They can teach you to sit with your feelings without trying to change them, fostering a sense of acceptance and resilience. Over time, these practices can help you embrace vulnerability as a strength, not a weakness, and diminish the hold of perfectionism on your life.

In the context of overcoming perfectionism, embracing vulnerability can be a game-changer. It allows you to connect authentically with others, build deeper relationships, and foster a sense of belonging and acceptance. By challenging the belief that vulnerability is a weakness, you can cultivate the courage to show up as your true self, imperfections and all. This shift can lead to a more balanced, fulfilling life where you are free from the constant pressure to be perfect and can instead focus on what truly matters.

From self-compassion to delegation and vulnerability, you now have key insights for softening perfectionism's hold on your everyday life. Bit by bit, you're learning to value growth and connection over rigid ideals. In the coming chapters, we'll discuss advanced practices and planning methods that lock in these healthier habits.

Chapter 10

Advanced Strategies

Y ou're sitting on your yoga mat, eyes closed, trying to focus on your breath.
Yet, your mind keeps drifting back to that presentation at work, the laundry
piling up at home, and an argument you had with a friend. The constant mental
chatter feels overwhelming, and you can't seem to find peace even in this quiet moment. But there is hope. Advanced mindfulness techniques can help you create
a deeper awareness and reduce the critical self-talk that fuels your perfectionism,
bringing a sense of relief to the overwhelming mental chatter.

10.1 Advanced Mindfulness and Meditation Techniques

Let's start with body scan meditations. This practice involves lying down in a
comfortable position and slowly bringing your attention to different parts of your
body, starting from your toes and moving up to your head. As you focus on each
area, notice any sensations without judgment. Feel the tension in your shoulders
or the warmth in your feet, acknowledging these sensations and releasing any
pent-up stress. This technique helps you tune into your body, grounding you in
the present moment and providing relief from the relentless pursuit of perfection.
Practicing this regularly can teach you to listen to your body's signals, allowing you to address stress and anxiety before they escalate. As you explore these
advanced methods, remember the CALM framework (chapter 6.1): Capture
anxious thoughts early, Accept that no practice is flawless, Let go of perfectionist
demands, and bring Mindfulness into each new technique.

Whether you start with a simple body scan or a loving-kindness practice, each exercise builds on the core mindfulness principle: noticing without judgment. Loving-kindness meditations can be truly transformative. Begin by sitting comfortably and focusing on your breath. When you feel centered, repeat phrases like "May I be happy, may I be healthy, may I be safe, may I live with ease." Start with yourself, then gradually extend these wishes to others—first to loved ones, then to acquaintances, and even to those with whom you have conflicts. This practice fosters compassion and empathy, reducing the harsh self-criticism that perfectionism thrives on. By regularly practicing loving-kindness meditation, you cultivate a kinder, more forgiving attitude towards yourself and others, creating a buffer against the critical inner voice that demands perfection.

For those looking to deepen their mindfulness practice, consider attending a mindfulness retreat. These immersive experiences, ranging from a weekend to several weeks, allow you to disconnect from daily stressors and immerse yourself in intensive mindfulness practices. Guided meditations, silent walks, and mindful eating are just a few of the activities you might engage in. Such retreats can provide profound insights and a lasting sense of peace, helping you understand the deeper layers of your perfectionism and how to manage it more effectively. The extended time for reflection and practice can lead to breakthroughs in how you approach your thoughts and behaviors.

Mindfulness is not just about formal practice; it's about integrating awareness into everyday life. Start by giving complete attention to mundane activities, like washing dishes or taking a shower. Notice the feel of the water, the scent of the soap, the sounds around you. This practice, often called "mindfulness of daily activities," empowers you to stay present and reduces the autopilot mode where perfectionist thoughts can take over. By staying mindful throughout your day, you learn to catch perfectionist impulses as they arise and gently redirect your focus to the present moment.

One powerful technique for managing perfectionist impulses is mindfulness of thoughts. Sit or lie down in a comfortable position and close your eyes. Take a few mindful breaths, then shift your attention to your mind. Observe your thoughts as they come and go without judging or getting caught up in them. When a perfectionist thought arises, acknowledge it by thinking, "Oh, here is a thought," and let it pass like a cloud drifting across the sky. Practicing this for a few minutes daily helps you recognize and release perfectionist thoughts, preventing them from taking root and escalating.

Lastly, the awareness of awareness practice can be particularly effective. This involves focusing on the silent observer or the awareness behind all forms—thoughts, sensations, emotions. Sit comfortably, close your eyes, and direct your attention to the awareness itself rather than the content of your thoughts. This practice can initially be challenging, but with time, it helps you detach from the constant stream of perfectionist thoughts and find a deeper sense of calm and clarity.

To deepen your practice, try incorporating these advanced techniques into your daily routine. Start small, perhaps with just a few minutes a day, and gradually increase the time as you become more comfortable. The key is consistency and patience. Over time, these practices can help you cultivate a more balanced, compassionate approach to life, reducing the grip of perfectionism and allowing you to embrace imperfection with grace.

10.2 The Balanced Life Pie: Allocating Energy Across Life's Domains

Imagine you're juggling multiple roles—parent, professional, friend, and more—each demanding time and energy. The Balanced Life Pie is a visual tool that helps you see whether your life's key areas (relationships, career, health, leisure, personal growth, spirituality, etc.) are in or out of balance. By spotting imbalances, such as a large portion of the pie being under-shaded or barely shaded, you can make changes and move toward a more fulfilling life.

Draw the Pie

- Start with a blank circle and divide it into slices—each slice stands for a major area of life (e.g., "Relationships," "Career," "Health," "Leisure," "Personal Growth," "Spirituality").

- Feel free to add or remove slices based on what matters most to you; it's your unique life map.

Shade Each Segment

In each slice, shade how satisfied you currently feel:

- Fully shaded for maximum satisfaction

- Partially shaded where you see room for improvement

- Barely shaded for severe neglect or dissatisfaction

This visual representation can be eye-opening. You might see that your "Career" slice is nearly full, while "Leisure" or "Health" is almost empty, indicating a potential source of stress or burnout.

Evaluate Satisfaction

Reflect on any slices that look unbalanced or under-shaded:

- If "Health" is low, do you need more exercise or better nutrition?

- If "Relationships" are under-served, could scheduling regular catch-ups help?

Awareness of these gaps helps you spot where perfectionism might steal time or energy from other important life areas.

<u>Adjust as Needed</u>

Once you've pinpointed the imbalances, make practical changes:

- If your career dominates, set boundaries or delegate tasks to free up personal time.

- If relationships are suffering, plan a weekly family dinner or monthly outing with friends.

- If you've neglected self-care, schedule short breaks or reintroduce a hobby you've shelved.

Remember that flexibility is key: life's demands shift, so stay open to revising your Balanced Life Pie. A big work project might consume more time temporarily, but it shouldn't become your default.

Regularly revisiting your Balanced Life Pie can keep you on track. Every few weeks, review each slice's shading and note any changes. This simple exercise helps ensure you're not sacrificing one critical area of life for another, nurturing a more harmonious balance in the long run.

10.3 Decision-Making Without Overthinking: A Step-by-Step Guide

You're facing a tough choice, whether about a career move, a relationship, or what to make for dinner. The options seem endless, and the more you think about it, the more paralyzed you feel. Overthinking can turn even simple decisions into monumental tasks, so let's break it down into manageable steps.

Decision-Making Checklist

1.Define the Decision

- Write down exactly what decision you need to make. This helps you focus and prevents your mind from wandering.

2. Brainstorm Options

- List all possible options without filtering any ideas. Let your thoughts flow freely.

3. Weigh Your Options

- Create a decision matrix with your options on one axis and criteria (such as cost, time, emotional impact, and long-term benefits) on the other.

Tip: You can use a scale, such as 1 to 5, 1 to 10, or even 1 to 100—whichever feels most intuitive.

- Assign each option a score based on how well it meets each criterion, then calculate the final score for clarity.

4. Trust Your Intuition

Your intuition acts as a mental shortcut that uses past experiences and feelings to guide you.

Now, let's talk about intuition. You've probably heard the phrase "trust your gut," and there's real wisdom in that. To strengthen this, try a simple exercise: close your eyes and imagine choosing each option. Pay attention to your immediate emotional response. Does one option make you feel excited or relieved? Does another make you feel anxious or tense? These gut reactions can provide valuable insights that logic alone might miss.

5. Set a Deadline

- Give yourself a specific timeframe (e.g., a few hours or a week) to decide. This prevents overthinking and forces commitment.

6. Finalize and Commit

- Choose an option, knowing that very few decisions are irreversible. If it turns out to be the wrong choice, you can adjust your course later.

Remember, the goal is to make decisions efficiently, not perfectly. Overthinking can lead to missed opportunities and unnecessary stress. By following this structured process, using tools like a decision matrix, trusting your intuition, and setting deadlines, you can make decisions with greater confidence and less anxiety.

10.4 The Art of Prioritization: Focusing on What Truly Matters

You wake up with a to-do list as long as your arm, and the day already feels overwhelming. How do you decide what truly needs your attention? Start by identifying and clarifying your key priorities. Think about your most important goals, both personal and professional. What aligns with your core values and long-term objectives? Jot these down. This exercise isn't just about listing tasks; it's about understanding what drives you and what you want to achieve.

Establishing routines can be a game-changer here. A structured framework for your day helps maintain focus on what really matters. Begin your morning with a consistent routine that includes a few minutes of planning and setting intentions. This simple act prioritizes your most critical tasks, ensuring you start the day with purpose and direction.

Remember to incorporate regular breaks into your schedule. Short, frequent pauses throughout the day are essential for maintaining productivity and mental clarity. These breaks aren't diversions; they're tools for self-care and focus. By stepping back periodically, you prevent burnout and remain energized to tackle your priorities effectively.

As your day winds down, use an evening routine to relax and reflect. Take time to evaluate your achievements and reassess your priorities for the next day. What worked well? Where did you face challenges? This reflective practice not only fosters growth but also keeps you aligned with your long-term goals. By ending your day with clarity, you're setting yourself up for success tomorrow.

Tools for Prioritization: Eisenhower Box and Pareto Principle

Now, let's explore two powerful tools to manage your priorities.

The **Eisenhower Box**, or urgent vs. important matrix, categorizes tasks into four quadrants:

1. **Urgent and Important (Do)**: Tasks that require immediate attention and have a significant impact.

2. **Important but Not Urgent (Plan)**: Tasks are essential for long-term goals but do not require immediate action.

3. **Urgent but Not Important (Delegate)**: Tasks requiring quick attention but not necessarily your involvement.

4. **Neither Urgent nor Important (Eliminate)**: Low-value distractions that don't contribute to your goals.

This tool ensures urgent tasks are handled efficiently while important but non-urgent tasks aren't neglected.

Pair this with the **Pareto Principle**, which emphasizes focusing on the 20% of tasks that yield 80% of the results. Start by identifying high-impact activities—those that create the most significant outcomes. Then, use the Eisenhower

Box to distinguish these critical tasks from less essential ones. Establishing routines around high-impact tasks ensures your energy is spent where it matters most.

Balancing and Reassessing Priorities

Balancing multiple priorities is challenging but achievable with the right mindset. Begin by categorizing tasks into urgent, important, and non-essential. Let go of tasks that don't significantly contribute to your primary goals. Flexible routines can help clarify what matters most, allowing for adjustments as priorities shift.

Regularly reassess your priorities to stay aligned with changing circumstances and goals. Remember, prioritization is an ongoing process, not a one-time task. By integrating prioritization into your daily routines, you're not just managing tasks—you're creating a life that reflects your values and aspirations.

This structured approach enhances clarity and focus and helps manage perfectionist tendencies, making it easier to embrace imperfection and stay centered on what truly matters.

10.5 The Role of Pets in Easing Perfectionist Tendencies

Imagine coming home after a long, stressful day. You're greeted by a wagging tail and your pet's enthusiastic, unconditional love. In that instant, the tension begins to melt away. Pets can provide incredible emotional support, acting as natural stress relievers. For individuals struggling with perfectionism, this emotional support is crucial. The simple act of petting a dog or watching a cat play can lower cortisol levels, reduce blood pressure, and boost serotonin—all of which contribute to a calmer, more relaxed state of mind. This emotional connection offers a soothing counterbalance to the relentless drive for perfection, reminding you that it's okay to let go and just be present.

Caring for a pet also establishes a routine that requires flexibility and adaptability—qualities that directly counteract perfectionistic rigidity. Feeding, walking, grooming, and playing with your pet requires a set schedule, but one that's forgiving of minor deviations. If you're late feeding your dog or miss a walk, the world doesn't end. This routine helps you learn to be more flexible and adaptable, understanding that not everything has to go according to plan. The predictability of pet care can provide a comforting structure. At the same time, the need for occasional adjustments teaches you to roll with the punches, reducing the anxiety associated with strict perfectionist standards.

Pets also teach us profound lessons about living in the moment and finding joy in simple pleasures. Watch a dog chase a ball or a cat bask in a sunny spot on the floor, and you'll see pure, unfiltered happiness. These moments can be incredibly grounding, offering a powerful reminder to appreciate the here and now. Pets don't worry about the future or dwell on past mistakes—they simply enjoy the present. This mindset can help shift your perspective away from perfectionist tendencies. By observing and mimicking your pet's behavior, you can learn to savor the small joys in life, reducing the pressure to constantly strive for unattainable ideals.

Moreover, pets offer a lesson in unconditional love and acceptance. They don't care if you had a bad day at work or if your performance wasn't perfect. For them, your presence is enough. This unconditional acceptance can be a powerful antidote to the self-criticism that plagues perfectionists. When you see yourself through your pet's eyes, it becomes easier to extend that same unconditional love and acceptance to yourself. You begin to realize that your worth isn't tied to your achievements but to who you are as a person.

Incorporating pets into your life can be a game-changer for managing perfectionism. They provide emotional support, help establish healthy routines, and teach valuable lessons about living in the moment and self-acceptance.

10.6 Creating a Personalized Perfectionism Management Plan

Imagine sitting down with a blank piece of paper, ready to draft a plan to help you manage your perfectionist tendencies. The first step is to outline the key components of your plan. Start by identifying your triggers. What situations or thoughts spark your perfectionist behaviors? Maybe it's work deadlines, social events, or even everyday tasks like cooking dinner. Recognizing these triggers is crucial because it allows you to anticipate and prepare for them.

Next, set realistic goals. Choose daily or weekly milestones over perfection. Breaking large projects into smaller targets prevents overwhelm.

Incorporate appropriate coping strategies. These might include mindfulness techniques, journaling, or talking to a trusted friend or therapist. Find what works best for you. Mindfulness can help you stay present and reduce anxiety, while journaling allows you to process your thoughts and emotions. Talking to someone can provide an outside perspective and emotional support.

Now, let's guide you through creating your personalized plan. Remember, this template is only a starting point. Below is a structured guide to help you outline your plan in a simple, actionable format. Feel free to modify, expand, or simplify each section to suit your unique needs and circumstances. There's no one-size-fits-all solution—this plan is yours to adapt as your journey unfolds.

Personalized Perfectionism Management Plan

Triggers (Situations that activate your perfectionism)	Emotional Response (How these triggers make you feel and why)	Goals (Breaking down big objectives into small steps)	Coping Strategies (Healthy ways to manage perfectionism and stress)
Work deadlines	"I feel anxious and overwhelmed because I fear making mistakes or not meeting expectations."	Complete project outline by Wednesday instead of trying to finish everything at once.	Practice deep breathing when overwhelmed.
Social events	"I dread interactions because I worry about being judged or saying the wrong thing."	Set a goal to stay present in conversations rather than overanalyzing everything.	Use positive self-talk before and after events.
Household chores	"I feel pressure to have everything perfectly clean, which makes me procrastinate."	Clean one room each day instead of trying to do everything at once.	Set a timer for short cleaning sessions and stop when time is up.
Giving presentations	"My heart races because I fear not being prepared enough or making mistakes."	Focus on communicating clearly rather than delivering a 'perfect' performance.	Rehearse but allow room for spontaneity— perfection is not required.
Receiving feedback	"I feel defensive and discouraged, as if criticism means I'm not good enough."	Shift focus to learning and improving rather than proving myself.	Write down feedback objectively and reframe it as an opportunity for growth.

As you put this plan into practice, remember that flexibility is key. Life is unpredictable, and adapting is part of the process. If a coping strategy isn't working, try something new. Maybe deep breathing doesn't help in high-stress moments, but a short walk or stretching exercise does. Similarly, if a particular goal is causing more stress than motivation, adjust it—break it down into smaller steps or extend the timeline. The goal is to make progress, not achieve perfection.

Regular check-ins keep your plan effective. Schedule time to review your progress—whether weekly, biweekly, or monthly. Ask yourself:

- Are my triggers becoming more manageable?

- Are my coping strategies helping?

- Do I need to tweak my goals to make them more realistic?

Use this self-reflection to make minor, meaningful adjustments, ensuring your plan remains practical and supportive rather than overwhelming.

Your Personalized Perfectionism Management Plan is a living document—it grows with you. By identifying triggers, setting realistic goals, and selecting effective coping strategies, you create a roadmap to balance and progress. With flexibility and regular self-assessment, this plan will evolve to meet your needs, supporting your well-being while helping you embrace imperfection.

We ventured beyond the basics—tackling deeper mindfulness, more nuanced decision-making, and the surprising stress relief that can come from pets or supportive networks. Now, let's draw inspiration from nature and industry leaders, finding how imperfection itself can spark innovative breakthroughs.

Chapter 11

Inspiration

You're sitting at your window, sipping a cup of coffee, and gazing at the chaotic beauty of a garden in full bloom. The flowers are not perfectly aligned, the leaves have holes from insects, and yet, it's breathtaking. This scene, filled with glorious imperfections, mirrors the natural world's resilience and adaptability. Nature doesn't strive for flawless symmetry or perfection; it thrives in its asymmetry and diversity, creating an environment of strength and beauty. This chapter is about drawing inspiration from the world around us, embracing imperfection, and finding beauty in the chaos.

For a perfectionist, nature's resilience offers a clear strategy: allow each "flaw" or unexpected turn to be a moment of adaptation rather than a source of self-criticism—just as an untidy forest floor nourishes future growth.

11.1 Embracing Imperfection: Lessons from Nature

Nature is a masterclass in the beauty of imperfection. Consider a forest where no two trees grow exactly alike. Some are tall and straight, while others twist and bend towards the light. The forest floor is a tapestry of fallen leaves, broken branches, and new growth pushing through the soil. It's not meticulously manicured, yet it thrives and supports a diverse ecosystem. This diversity and resilience are precisely what makes it so robust. Just like these trees, our imperfections and unique paths contribute to our strength and beauty. Embracing our natural, uneven growth can lead to a more fulfilling life.

The Japanese philosophy of Wabi-sabi offers a profound way to appreciate this kind of beauty. Rooted in ancient tea ceremonies, Wabi-sabi celebrates imperfection, impermanence, and the incomplete. It finds beauty in the simplest and most humble objects and experiences. Imagine a handcrafted pottery cup with a slight crack or a piece of weathered wood with a rich patina. These imperfections tell a story of time and use, adding depth and character. Wabi-sabi encourages us to see our own cracks and wear them as part of our unique beauty, promoting mindfulness and a deeper appreciation of life's intricacies.

Engaging with nature can be a powerful way to physically and mentally experience these benefits. Consider hiking through a forest trail, where each step brings you closer to the natural world. Notice the uneven path, the fallen leaves, and the way the sunlight filters through the canopy. This immersion in nature's imperfections can help you appreciate your own. Gardening is another excellent way to connect with nature. Planting seeds, nurturing their growth, and accepting that not every plant will flourish as expected mirrors the unpredictability of life. Each bloom and each failure is a lesson in resilience and acceptance.

Nature photography is another activity that can reinforce these lessons. Capturing the raw beauty of landscapes, animals, and plants in their natural state can shift your focus from seeking perfection to appreciating what is. The asymmetry of a tree, the rough texture of the bark, the vibrant yet imperfect flower petals—all these elements create a stunning tapestry of life. Through a camera lens, you can learn to see and celebrate the beauty in the imperfect, applying this perspective to your own life.

Ecosystems thrive through diversity and adaptation, teaching us valuable lessons about resilience. In a healthy ecosystem, every species plays a role, and the system's strength lies in its diversity. If one species faces a challenge, others can adapt and fill the gap, maintaining balance. This principle applies to our lives as well.

Embracing diversity in our skills, experiences, and perspectives makes us more adaptable and resilient. Just as ecosystems benefit from a variety of species, we benefit from our myriad experiences and the different facets of our personalities.

Nature Journal Exercise

Take a moment to engage directly with the natural world. Spend some time outside, whether it's in a local park, your backyard, or a hiking trail. Bring a journal with you and observe the details around you. Write down what you see, hear, and feel. Pay special attention to the imperfections—the crooked branches, the uneven ground, the varied colors and textures. Reflect on how these imperfections contribute to the overall beauty and resilience of the scene. Then, consider how your own imperfections add to the richness of your life. Use this exercise to cultivate a deeper appreciation for the natural world and your place within it.

Nature's lessons extend beyond the physical environment to philosophical concepts. The idea of "ma" in Wabi-sabi represents space or emptiness, highlighting the significance of pauses and silence. In our fast-paced lives, we often overlook the value of these pauses. Yet, just as a tree needs space to grow, we need moments of stillness to reflect and rejuvenate. Embracing "ma" means appreciating the spaces between our actions, the quiet moments that allow us to process and heal. It's in these pauses that we find clarity and insight, fostering a more mindful and content existence.

By incorporating the principles of Wabi-sabi into our daily lives, we can learn to embrace imperfection and find beauty in the unexpected. You can also apply the CALM method from Chapter 6.1 -Capture self-doubt, Accept natural flaws, Let go of rigid ideals, and practice Mindfulness—to turn these real-world inspirations into everyday habits. This mindset encourages us to slow down, observe, and appreciate the world around us. It invites us to find joy in the simplest aspects of existence, counterbalancing the modern pursuit of perfection. Whether it's through mindful observation, creative activities, or philosophical reflection, embracing imperfection opens the door to a more fulfilling and balanced life.

As you continue to explore these concepts, remember that nature's beauty lies in its imperfection and resilience. Just as a garden flourishes with diverse plants and varied growth, your life can thrive by embracing your unique path and imperfections. Let the natural world be your guide, teaching you to find strength and beauty in the chaos and unpredictability of life.

11.2 Innovating Through Imperfection: Lessons from Industry Leaders

Imagine you're working on a project, and nothing seems to be going right. The idea you were so excited about isn't panning out, and frustration is building. It's easy to see these moments as failures, but what if they're actually stepping stones to something greater? Imperfection and failure often pave the way for innovation. When we embrace and learn from mistakes, we open the door to progress and creativity. This mindset shift can transform how we approach challenges in any field.

Consider the words of Henry Ford, a pioneer in the automotive industry: "Failure is simply the opportunity to begin again, this time more intelligently." Ford understood that each setback was a learning experience, a chance to refine and improve. Similarly, Winston Churchill once remarked: "Success is stumbling from failure to failure with no loss of enthusiasm." These quotes remind us that even the most accomplished figures have faced numerous failures on their path to success. They didn't let these setbacks deter them; instead, they used them as fuel to keep moving forward.

"Success is stumbling from failure to failure with no loss of enthusiasm."

Winston Churchill

In the tech industry, Apple is a prime example of turning failure into groundbreaking success. In the early 1990s, Apple launched the Newton MessagePad, an ambitious attempt at creating a personal digital assistant. Despite its innovative concept, the Newton was plagued with issues and ultimately failed in the market. However, Apple didn't let this setback define them. Instead, they learned from their mistakes, refining their approach to technology and design. This perseverance led to the development of the iPhone, a revolutionary product that transformed the tech industry. Steve Jobs, Apple's visionary leader, once said, "The people who are crazy enough to think they can change the world are the ones who do." This mindset of embracing failure and pushing boundaries is what drove Apple to innovate and succeed. For perfectionists, Apple's story shows that an initial "failure" can be a catalyst for refining your approach—seeing early missteps as stepping stones for growth rather than evidence of inadequacy.

In the world of design, IDEO is renowned for its approach to innovation through imperfection. The company employs a concept known as rapid prototyping, where early failures are seen as essential parts of the creative process. By quickly building and testing prototypes, they identify flaws and make improvements in real time. This iterative process allows for continuous learning and innovation. Tim Brown, CEO of IDEO, captures this philosophy perfectly: "Fail often to succeed sooner." By viewing mistakes as opportunities for growth, IDEO fosters a culture of creativity and resilience.

Entrepreneurship is another field where embracing imperfection can lead to remarkable success. Take Airbnb, for instance. When the founders, Brian Chesky and Joe Gebbia, first pitched their idea of an online marketplace for short-term lodging, they faced multiple rejections. Investors were skeptical, and the concept seemed too unconventional. However, Chesky and Gebbia believed in their vision and persevered through the setbacks. Reid Hoffman, co-founder of LinkedIn, once said, "If you are not embarrassed by the first version of your product, you've launched too late." This quote rings true for Airbnb, whose early iterations were far from perfect. Yet, through persistence and learning from their mistakes, they refined their platform and built a global company that revolution-ized the travel industry. A perfectionist might have delayed launching indefinitely, but Airbnb's journey reminds us that a "no-need-for-flawless" approach can be a vital step toward genuine innovation and impact.

The power of imperfection in driving innovation is evident. It's not just a hur-dle to overcome but a valuable tool that can lead to growth and creativity. By embracing our imperfections and viewing them as opportunities for learning, we can unlock our potential and achieve remarkable things. Ultimately, it's the willingness to take risks, make mistakes, and learn from them that fuels true innovation.

Nature's quiet resilience and innovators' willingness to fail reveal how embracing imperfection drives creativity and resilience. In the final chapter, we'll combine everything you've learned to redefine success and build a more peaceful self-im-age—one that thrives on actual progress, not flawless performance.

Keeping the Calm Alive

Now that you have the tools to break free from perfectionism and embrace a more balanced, joyful life, it's time to help others do the same.

Simply by sharing your honest thoughts about this book, you can guide other perfectionists toward the support they need. Your review on Amazon will help them see that they are not alone—and that there is a way forward.

Thank you for being part of this journey. The path to self-acceptance and happiness grows stronger when we share what we've learned, and you're helping me do just that.

>>> For ebook, Click here to leave your review on Amazon

Or (for paperback) scan this QR code :

Chapter 12

Moving Forward: Building a New Self-Image

Y ou're flipping through an old photo album, and a picture catches your eye. It's from a time when you were trying so hard to meet everyone else's expectations. You remember the stress, the anxiety, the constant feeling that you were never quite good enough. But what if you could redefine what success means to you? What if you could move beyond those old, suffocating metrics and find a new way to measure your worth?

12.1 Redefining Success: Metrics Beyond Perfection

We've all been there, striving for the perfect job, the perfect house, the perfect life. Society often equates success with wealth, status, and flawless performance. But these traditional definitions can leave you feeling empty and constantly chasing an unattainable ideal. Take a moment to think about someone like J.K. Rowling. Before Harry Potter became a global phenomenon, she was a single mother living on welfare. Success, for her, wasn't about wealth or status; it was about telling a story she was passionate about, and she redefined it on her own terms. Her journey from struggling writer to beloved author shows that success doesn't always follow a straight line. For perfectionists, Rowling's journey illustrates that genuine success may involve early setbacks and imperfect drafts—embracing those missteps can lead to astonishing achievements.

So, how do you develop personal success criteria that resonate with your true self? Start by thinking about what really matters to you. Is it balance between work and personal life? Is it personal growth, fulfillment, or well-being? These values can guide you in setting goals that are meaningful and achievable. Imagine success as a garden, where each plant represents a different aspect of your life. Instead of focusing on one perfect flower, you cultivate a variety of plants that together create a beautiful, balanced garden. This approach shifts the focus from perfection to fulfillment.

To help you redefine and set meaningful success goals, take a moment for reflection. Think about the key areas of your life—career, relationships, health, personal growth, and leisure. Ask yourself:

- Which of these areas feels most fulfilling right now?

- Where do you feel something is missing or out of balance?

- What small, intentional changes could you make to bring greater harmony across these areas?

Consider writing down your thoughts in a journal. For each area, list one thing you're proud of and one area where you'd like to grow. Focus on what brings you joy and aligns with your values rather than trying to meet external expectations.

This reflective practice helps you gain clarity on where to direct your energy and how to prioritize your time. Over time, this process can guide you toward a more balanced and fulfilling life grounded in what truly matters to you.

Reflect on your current definitions of success. Are they rooted in societal expectations, or do they align with what truly brings you joy and fulfillment? Redefining success isn't about lowering your standards; it's about shifting your focus to what genuinely matters to you. It's about recognizing that balance, growth, and well-being are just as valuable—if not more so—than any external accolade.

As you move forward, remember that success is a deeply personal journey. It's about creating a life that feels right for you, not one that looks perfect from the outside. If you sense old perfectionist urges creeping back, recall the CALM method from Chapter 6.1— Capture those self-critical thoughts, Accept that life can be messy, Let go of unattainable standards, and stay Mindful of what truly matters. By redefining your metrics of success, you can build a new self-image grounded in authenticity, resilience, and true happiness.

12.2 Building Resilience and Celebrating Small Wins

Imagine you're at your desk, overwhelmed by a mountain of tasks. Suddenly, you find yourself slipping back into old habits—working late into the night, criticizing every minor mistake, or avoiding tasks altogether because they don't seem perfect. This is what a perfectionist relapse looks like. During stressful times, it's easy to revert to these patterns, but recognizing them is the first step to overcoming them. Understanding that these relapses are a natural part of the process helps you approach them with self-compassion rather than frustration.

Recognizing and celebrating small wins is crucial in building resilience against these relapses. Celebrating small victories can shift your focus from what's missing to what's been achieved, reinforcing positive behavior. Picture this: You've managed to complete a task earlier than expected. Instead of diving into the next one immediately, take a moment to acknowledge this achievement. Small wins provide the motivation and confidence needed to resist the pull of perfectionist tendencies, helping you stay on track. They act as building blocks, creating a foundation of positive reinforcement that makes it easier to bounce back from setbacks.

There are practical ways to acknowledge and celebrate progress. Keeping a journal of daily achievements can be incredibly empowering. At the end of each day, jot down three things you accomplished, no matter how small. This simple act of recognition can shift your mindset from focusing on what's left to do to

appreciating what's been done. Rewarding yourself for meeting milestones is another effective strategy. Treat yourself to a favorite snack, a walk in the park, or a relaxing activity when you complete a significant task. Sharing your successes with others can also provide added support and encouragement. Whether it's a quick text to a friend or a celebratory dinner with loved ones, sharing your wins helps reinforce the positive behavior and builds a supportive network around you
.

Celebrating small wins in your daily routine can build long-term resilience against setbacks. This regular recognition of progress helps maintain momentum and fosters a positive outlook. It's essential to recognize early signs of relapse, such as increased stress, negative self-talk, or avoidance behaviors. When you notice these signs, use small wins to regain your footing. For instance, if you're feeling overwhelmed at work, break down your tasks into smaller, manageable steps and celebrate each one you complete. This approach not only makes the workload feel less daunting but also keeps you motivated.

By consistently celebrating even the smallest wins, you build a sustainable, positive mindset that values growth and effort over unattainable perfection. This shift in perspective can transform how you navigate challenges, making it easier to maintain progress and stay resilient in the face of setbacks.

12.3 The Power of Gratitude in Overcoming Perfectionism

Imagine you're at the end of a long day, mentally cataloging everything that didn't go as planned. The report you turned in was good but not great. The dinner you cooked was tasty but not perfect. This relentless focus on what's missing or imperfect can be crippling. That's where gratitude steps in. Shifting your focus from what's absent to what is present can dramatically improve your mental well-being. Gratitude helps you appreciate the abundance in your life, reducing the tendency to overanalyze and stress over imperfections. Focusing on what's right can create a more balanced and optimistic outlook.

Incorporating gratitude into your daily routine doesn't require a grand overhaul of your life. Start simple. Keep a gratitude journal by your bedside and jot down three things you're grateful for each night before bed. These can be as small as a warm cup of coffee in the morning or a kind word from a colleague. Sharing grateful thoughts with loved ones is another powerful practice. Over dinner, you might ask each family member to share one thing they're grateful for that day. These small acts of gratitude can build a reservoir of positive emotions that buffer against the daily stresses and imperfections we all face.

Studies show the profound impact of gratitude on well-being. Studies have shown that regular gratitude practices can decrease stress and increase resilience. For instance, a study published by Harvard Summer School found that acknowledging small wins and practicing gratitude can significantly reduce the fear of failure and clarify direction. This, in turn, increases the likelihood of future success. Counting your blessings rather than your burdens can elevate your mindset, helping you approach challenges with a more positive and resilient attitude. This shift can be transformative, especially for those who struggle with perfectionism.

Gratitude can also extend beyond personal practices to community involvement. Volunteering your time or resources to help others can reinforce feelings of gratitude and connection. Engaging in community service or support groups not only benefits those you help but also strengthens your own sense of purpose and fulfillment. It's a powerful reminder that you are part of a larger community that can provide comfort and support. Acts of kindness, whether through formal volunteering or simple daily gestures, can cultivate a deeper sense of gratitude and well-being.

The mental health benefits of gratitude are extensive. Practicing gratitude helps regulate emotions, elevates your mindset, and fosters connections with others. It can also motivate better outcomes by encouraging health-promoting behaviors and inspiring prosocial actions. Feeling grateful makes you more likely to handle life with care, attentiveness, and consciousness. This emotional shift can anchor you back to a sense of inner peace, protecting you from the stress and anxiety that often accompany perfectionism. Keeping a gratitude journal, appreciating intangible aspects of life, honoring the present moment, and performing acts of kindness are practical steps you can take to weave gratitude into the fabric of your daily life.

12.4 Fostering Authentic Connections

You're at a gathering surrounded by people. Yet, you feel isolated because you're caught up in trying to present a perfect version of yourself. This is where the importance of social connections comes into play. A network of supportive, understanding friends and family can be a game-changer in overcoming perfectionism. These connections provide the emotional resilience needed to maintain progress, offering a safe space to be your true self without the fear of judgment. When you feel supported, it's easier to keep perfectionist tendencies at bay and focus on what truly matters—genuine human connection.

Building and sustaining authentic relationships requires mutual understanding, acceptance, and support. It's about creating bonds where both parties can be vulnerable and open. Think about the friends you confide in, the ones who know your quirks and flaws but love you anyway. These are the relationships worth nurturing. Encourage open conversations about your struggles and listen with empathy when others share theirs. This mutual vulnerability fosters deeper connections and helps dismantle the walls that perfectionism builds. It's not about setting boundaries but about creating a space where it's safe to be imperfect.

Maintaining these authentic relationships can significantly aid in personal growth and resisting perfectionist tendencies. Your connections act as a support network, keeping you accountable and resilient. Imagine a friend who gently reminds you to take a break when you're overworking or celebrates your small wins with you. These interactions not only provide emotional support but also reinforce positive behaviors. Leveraging your social network in this way helps you stay grounded and focused on your personal growth rather than getting lost in the pursuit of perfection. Your friends and loved ones can offer perspectives and advice you might not see on your own, helping you navigate challenges more effectively.

Consider the role of vulnerability in these relationships. Embracing vulnerability means sharing your fears, mistakes, and uncertainties with those you trust. It's a powerful way to connect on a deeper level, showing that you don't have to be perfect to be loved and respected. This shared vulnerability builds a foundation of trust and empathy, allowing both parties to grow and learn from each other. By being open about your imperfections, you encourage others to do the same, creating a cycle of authenticity and support that benefits everyone involved.

In these authentic connections, you'll find the strength to face your perfectionist tendencies head-on. Your friends and family become mirrors, reflecting your flaws, strengths, and progress. They remind you that it's okay to be human, to make mistakes, and to grow from them. This reinforcement of your worth, independent of your achievements, helps shift your mindset from perfectionism to acceptance and growth.

12.5 Embracing a Lifetime of Imperfect Happiness

Imagine you're getting ready for an event, running through a mental checklist of everything that needs to be flawless. The dress, the presentation, even your smile. Yet, despite your best efforts, something always feels off. True happiness doesn't lie in these perfect moments but in embracing life's natural imperfections. When you let go of the need for perfection, you create space for genuine contentment. Think about the last time something didn't go as planned but ended up being unexpectedly memorable—like a rainy picnic that turned into a cozy indoor gathering. Often, it's these imperfect moments that bring the most joy.

Different cultures and philosophies have long celebrated this idea. The Japanese philosophy of Wabi-sabi finds beauty in imperfection and transience. Hygge, the Danish concept of coziness and comfort, encourages savoring simple, everyday pleasures like a warm cup of tea or a soft blanket. Meanwhile, Stoicism teaches us to accept what we cannot control and focus on how we respond. Together, these philosophies offer practical ways to embrace life's messiness and find a more profound sense of fulfillment.

Wabi-sabi reminds us to appreciate the natural wear and tear of life. Look around your home—maybe you'll spot a chipped mug, a frayed book, or a worn-out chair. Instead of seeing these as flaws, reflect on the stories they hold and how their imperfections make them unique. Hygge invites us to create cozy, joy-filled moments. Light some candles, curl up with a favorite book, or simply enjoy a peaceful evening with loved ones. And Stoicism encourages us to focus on what we can control. If you've recently felt overwhelmed by a situation, consider how you might reframe it using Stoic principles to find peace in the face of uncertainty.

These philosophies, taken together, guide us toward acceptance, presence, and resilience. To explore this further, pick one philosophy and focus on it for a week. Perhaps you choose to find beauty in imperfection through Wabi-sabi, embrace simple pleasures with Hygge, or practice emotional resilience using Stoicism. Notice how this shift in mindset changes your perspective and enriches your daily li fe.

For long-term contentment, it's essential to set realistic expectations. Perfectionism often comes from holding ourselves to impossible standards, so take a moment to identify areas where you can ease those demands. What if you gave yourself permission to appreciate things as they are? When challenges arise, instead of fixating on what went wrong, focus on what you learned from the experience. Each obstacle is an opportunity to grow.

Building resilience doesn't have to mean taking dramatic leaps. Start small by stepping out of your comfort zone in manageable ways—a new hobby, a conversation you've been avoiding, or simply saying "yes" to an unexpected opportunity. Each time you do, reflect on what you gained from the experience. Over time, these small steps will strengthen your ability to navigate life's imperfections gracefully and confidently.

Finally, integrate these ideas into your daily routine through gratitude and mindfulness. Each day, jot down three things you're grateful for, paying attention to the small, overlooked details. When you catch yourself being overly critical, pause, take a deep breath, and gently shift your focus back to the present moment. Savor the small pleasures—whether it's a walk in the park, a favorite meal, or a quiet moment of reflection.

Accepting life's imperfections and focusing on what truly matters can cultivate a lasting sense of contentment. Happiness isn't about chasing perfection; it's about embracing life as it is, finding beauty in its flaws, and building a resilient mindset that carries you through life's ups and downs.

12.6 The Legacy of Imperfection: What We Leave Behind

Think about legacy. Traditional views often tie it to flawless achievements and material success. But what if legacy was more about who we are and how we connect with others? By embracing our imperfections, we create a legacy of authenticity and growth. Consider someone like Maya Angelou. Her life was marked by struggles and imperfections, yet she built a legacy of resilience, wisdom, and empathy. Her willingness to share her vulnerabilities inspired many to embrace their own, showing that our greatest impact often comes from our authentic selves.

Embracing vulnerability is like opening a window to your soul. When you share your struggles and flaws, you allow others to do the same. This creates a ripple effect, fostering a culture of openness and empathy. Imagine your friend confiding in you about their fears, feeling less alone because you've shared yours too. This kind of connection can be deeply healing and transformative, making people feel more connected and less isolated in their struggles. It's a powerful way to leave a legacy of compassion and understanding.

Failures and imperfections aren't just setbacks; they're opportunities for growth. When you acknowledge your failures, you show others that it's okay to make mistakes. This can encourage them to view their challenges as opportunities to learn and grow. Think of Thomas Edison, who famously said, "I have not failed. I've just found 10,000 ways that won't work." By normalizing imperfection, you leave a legacy that values resilience and continuous learning over unattainable perfection. This mindset can inspire others to take risks and pursue their passions without fear of failure.

Embracing imperfections also fosters authentic relationships. When you accept your own flaws, you become more accepting of others. This creates deeper, more meaningful connections based on mutual understanding and acceptance. Imagine a community where people support each other without judgment, where imperfections are seen as part of the beauty of human experience. Such a legacy of authenticity and compassion can influence how future generations interact and support one another, creating a more empathetic world.

Our legacy is shaped not just by grand achievements but by everyday actions that reflect our values. Acts of kindness, understanding, and acceptance of imperfections in daily life contribute to a lasting impact on those around us. Whether offering a listening ear, helping a neighbor, or simply being kind to yourself, these small actions add up. They create a ripple effect extending beyond your immediate circle, influencing how others behave and interact.

Passing on the message of embracing imperfection is crucial. Share your experiences and lessons learned with others, whether through storytelling, mentoring, or simply leading by example. This helps perpetuate a culture that values imperfection as a part of the human experience. Imagine the impact you can have by showing others that it's okay to be imperfect, that it's okay to be human. This kind of legacy can inspire generations to come, creating a world that values authenticity, resilience, and compassion.

The most meaningful legacies are those that embrace and celebrate imperfection. Focus on the positive impact you can have on others by being authentic, resilient, and compassionate. This legacy, built on the gifts of imperfection, will resonate with future generations and leave a lasting imprint on the world.

By combining self-compassion, honest reflection, and a newly flexible sense of success, you're dismantling old perfectionist patterns. In conclusion, we'll gather these threads to highlight how each step forward—no matter how small—expands the freedom to live authentically and at ease.

Conclusion

Y ou take a deep breath as you glance at your to-do list. It's still there—tasks waiting, expectations looming—but something has shifted. Instead of feeling trapped by the weight of perfection, you recognize progress over flawlessness. You've learned that completion, not perfection, is the goal. With each step forward, you release the need for unattainable standards and embrace the freedom of 'good enough.

Throughout this book, we've explored the deep roots of perfectionism and its pervasive impact on various aspects of life. We started by understanding what perfectionism is and how it can mask itself as ambition, leading to chronic dissatisfaction and mental health struggles. We differentiated between perfectionism and excellence and discussed how a growth mindset can help alleviate the pressures of perfectionism.

We delved into personal relationships, showing how perfectionism can create unrealistic expectations and strain connections with loved ones. We explored strategies for fostering acceptance and appreciation in romantic relationships, balanced parenting approaches, and building friendships rooted in self-compassion. We also looked at setting boundaries with family to maintain healthy and supportive interactions.

In your professional life, we examined how perfectionism impacts career choices and job performance. We discussed the importance of aligning career choices with personal values, managing perfectionism in leadership and team dynamics, and strategies for handling criticism and feedback. Moreover, we offered tools for achieving balanced productivity and integrating self-care into your work routine.

As you navigated through the different stages of life, from childhood to adulthood and into the golden years, you learned how perfectionism manifests uniquely at each stage. We provided tailored strategies to manage perfectionism across these stages, emphasizing the continuous learning process and the importance of self-compassion.

The heart of this journey is the realization that embracing imperfection brings liberation and peace. Accepting and celebrating imperfection in all aspects of life leads to a more authentic, fulfilled, and happy existence. This shift in mindset is the foundation for ongoing personal growth and happiness.

Now, I challenge you to continue applying the book's insights as part of your life-long journey of self-improvement and acceptance. Over the next month, commit to practicing one strategy from this book daily. Track your progress and reflect on how these changes impact your well-being and relationships. Remember, this is a continuous process, every step forward counts.

Consider this book not an endpoint but a stepping stone in your ongoing journey of self-discovery and personal development. Explore further resources and communities that align with the teachings here, deepening your understanding and application of the strategies provided. Seek support from friends, family, or professionals when struggling with perfectionism. Shared experiences and collective growth can be powerful tools for overcoming challenges and fostering a sense of belonging.

I want to express my deepest gratitude for your commitment to this journey. It takes courage to confront perfectionism and work towards overcoming it. Celebrate your progress, no matter how small, and continue embracing your imperfections with kindness and understanding.

As Elizabeth Gilbert beautifully said, "Embrace the glorious mess that you are." Carry this message forward in your life, knowing that each step you take towards self-acceptance and happiness is a step worth celebrating.

Remember, the journey is ongoing, but every moment of growth and self-compassion brings you closer to a life of balance and fulfillment. Embrace the beauty of your imperfections, and let the limitless potential for growth and happiness guide you forward. You have the power to create a life that feels right for you, one imperfect, beautiful step at a time.

May you carry forward the grace to see that imperfection isn't a weakness but a sign of life's natural flow. With each chapter's lessons in mind, let compassion, courage, and curiosity be your compass as you embrace this radiant, imperfect journey.

Want more support on your journey?

Whether you're navigating parenting challenges, emotional growth, or personal transformation; you're not alone.

I've written other books designed to guide and uplift you, whatever stage you're in.

Explore all my titles here:

or Click here

You may be just one book away from the insight or comfort you've been needing.

Available in print, Ebook, and audiobook formats.

References

AntiLoneliness. (n.d.). *Perfectionism: From toxic to healthy.* Retrieved from https://www.antiloneliness.com/perfectionism-toxic-healthy.html

BetterUp. (n.d.). *All-or-nothing thinking: 3 ways to stop throwing in the towel.* Retrieved from https://www.betterup.com/blog/all-or-nothing-thinking

Brainz Magazine. (n.d.). *Overcome perfectionism – A guide for leaders.* Retrieved from https://www.brainzmagazine.com/post/overcome-perfectionism-a-guide-for-leaders

Brown, B. (2013, April 21). *How vulnerability can make our lives better.* Forbes. Retrieved from https://www.forbes.com/sites/danschawbel/2013/04/21/brene-brown-how-vulnerability-can-make-our-lives-better/

Calm. (n.d.). *How to stop being a perfectionist: 6 tips.* Retrieved from https://www.calm.com/blog/how-to-stop-being-a-perfectionist

Dalry Rose Digital. (n.d.). *The power of authenticity: Why viewers prefer unpolished content over ads.* Retrieved from https://www.dalryrosedigital.co.uk/single-post/the-power-of-authenticity-why-viewers-prefer-unpolished-content-over-ads

Dweck, C. (n.d.). *Carol Dweck: A summary of growth and fixed mindsets.* Retrieved from https://fs.blog/carol-dweck-mindset/

Earn Spend Live. (2023, August). *Mind matters: 7 hobbies to cultivate mental clarity and resilience*. Retrieved from https://earnspendlive.com/2023/08/mind-matters-7-hobbies-to-cultivate-mental-clarity-and-resilience/

E! News. (n.d.). *Celebrities who own their beautiful "imperfections"*. Retrieved from https://www.eonline.com/photos/14948/celebrities-who-own-their-beautiful-imperfections

Forbes. (2022, April 3). *Perfectionism is bad for your career: 3 most important things to know*. Retrieved from https://www.forbes.com/sites/tracybrower/2022/04/03/perfectionism-is-bad-for-your-career-3-most-important-things-to-know/

Forbes Health. (n.d.). *The mental health benefits of gratitude*. Retrieved from https://www.forbes.com/health/mind/mental-health-benefits-of-gratitude/

Focus People. (2024, April 10). *Balancing productivity and well-being: 10 tips for success*. Retrieved from https://www.focuspeople.com/2024/04/10/balancing-productivity-and-well-being-10-tips-for-success/

Harvard Summer School. (n.d.). *Why celebrating small wins matters*. Retrieved from https://summer.harvard.edu/blog/why-celebrating-small-wins-matters/

LinkedIn. (n.d.). *How to handle criticism with emotional intelligence*. Retrieved from https://www.linkedin.com/advice/3/how-do-you-handle-feedback-criticism-emotional

Mayo Clinic. (n.d.). *Chronic stress puts your health at risk*. Retrieved from https://www.mayoclinic.org/healthy-lifestyle/stress-management/in-depth/stress/art-20046037

Medical News Today. (n.d.). *The effects of perfectionism on mental and physical health*. Retrieved from https://www.medicalnewstoday.com/articles/323323

Newport Academy. (n.d.). *How perfectionism in children impacts mental health.* Retrieved from https://www.newportacademy.com/resources/empowering-teens/perfectionism-in-children/

NIH News in Health. (2018, February). *The power of pets.* Retrieved from https://newsinhealth.nih.gov/2018/02/power-pets

NYU Steinhardt. (n.d.). *A closer look at the perfectionism construct.* Retrieved from https://wp.nyu.edu/steinhardt-appsych_opus/problematizing-perfectionism-a-closer-look-at-the-perfectionism-construct/

Penn Medicine. (2019, November). *Dis-like: How social media feeds into perfectionism.* Retrieved from https://www.pennmedicine.org/news/news-blog/2019/november/dis-like-how-social-media-feeds-into-perfectionism

Positive Psychology. (n.d.). *Fostering self-forgiveness: 25 powerful techniques and strategies.* Retrieved from https://positivepsychology.com/self-forgiveness/

ProQuest. (n.d.). *Cultural differences in perfectionism: A comparison.* Retrieved from https://www.proquest.com/scholarly-journals/cultural-differences-perfectionism-comparison/docview/195180531/se-2

Verywell Mind. (n.d.). *How to deal with perfectionism in relationships.* Retrieved from https://www.verywellmind.com/dealing-with-perfectionism-in-a-relationship-5226092

Wondermind. (n.d.). *Setting boundaries with family is hard—Here's how to do it.* Retrieved from https://www.wondermind.com/article/setting-boundaries-with-family/

Printed in Dunstable, United Kingdom

76321618R00087